CONQUERING CORPORATE CIRCUS

College Campus to Corporate Corridors

Pradeep Chhabra

Author of Best Seller UNCORK YOURSELF NOT BOTTLES

Foreword by

Himanshu Kapania
Vice Chairman Grasim Industries Ltd. (Aditya Birla Group)

ISBN 978-93-5346-658-9

Typeset at Script Makers, 19, A1-B, DDA Market, Paschim Vihar, New Delhi 110063, and cover design at Script Makers.

Your attitude not your aptitude will determine your altitude.

—Zig Ziglar

*Dedicated to my late parents
Mrs. Sudarshan Chhabra and Mr. Som Dutt Chhabra,
who taught me the joy of giving.*

Miss you every moment!

Foreword

This is the second book by Pradeep Chhabra post the huge success of his first book titled UNCORK YOURSELF NOT BOTTLES on corporate life and careers. His ability to flag the relevant issues on work related environment, culture and behaviour has been applauded by many. Several corporates have positioned the book in their libraries and have also used it as a giveaway in training programs.

Corporate life is undergoing a change from the past due to rapid strides in technology, its adaption and resultant impacts on the working environment. This includes Artificial Intelligence, Internet of things, Block chain, Digital currencies, Mixed reality augmented and virtual, Smart phones, Cloud computing and many more such things. Rapidly changing global scene on economic policies of individual nations of moving from global to local, from exports to domestic consumption is further a matter of concern. Tweets by President of the United States (POTUS) can destroy or enhance the global financial and commodities markets in a matter of seconds. Inflow of funds can reverse from one direction to other. You don't need guns any more just a tweet of 140 words can change the economic landscape of a nation. Words in the tweets can do many things like inspire, connect, care, cry, dare, laugh and many more life impacting events. Your personal brand, your professional brand, your product brand can be made or destroyed in a matter of minutes and that too with a few words. Customer service, Customer feedback, asking for orders, Marketing, Sales pitch and many more are done on Twitter. Look at the speed of actions and spread of information across the globe. New language of signs like #, @, * & Emojis is already in place. Information is around in abundance and flies thick and fast. You need to differentiate between real and fake. Hoarding information real or fake is a thing of past and the adage, information is power is no longer valid.

WhatsApp and messenger have nearly replaced emails and SMSs. All stake holders need to readjust to the new realities on the horizon. This includes you, your colleague, your boss, your customer, your customer's customer and on personal front, your spouse, your kids and your extended and immediate family as well. While millennials may not find any difficulty as it is their first step, persons with earlier background may find it more challenging to adjust.

It will need change of belief system. It will need change of attitude. It will need change of behaviour on all fronts, be it personal, professional, social and financial. What you thought yesterday to be right may not be true today. Are you ready for such rapid changes in your thought process? Are you ready to accept mistakes which you may have made in the past?

Many issues relevant for day to day work in personal, professional, economic, financial, and social life are detailed in the book. In case you are about to start your professional life or you are a practising manager and already in service for few years and of course those leading the teams are all going to immensely benefit from this book. As earlier, this book Conquering Corporate Circus is quick to read, understand, retain and recall what has been read. Hopefully it will answer many questions which come often in a reader's mind in personal and professional life.

Himanshu Kapania

Vice Chairman
Grasim Industries Ltd.
(Flagship Company of Aditya Birla group)
Mumbai
Jan 2019

About the Author

 Pradeep Chhabra is an astute and result oriented professional with + 4 decades (1976- 2017) of experience both in the Public and Private sector in managing business and business development activities in downstream of Oil, Gas and Petrochemicals. Born and brought up in Delhi, Mechanical engineer by education, Marketer at heart, lives with his wife, Meenakshi and son, Siddhant. Enjoys listening to music, loves travelling and reading non-fiction. He is a firm believer in raising the professional and personal standards of others. He can be reached at

www.pradeepchhabra.com
pradeepchhabra@hotmail.com,
pradeep.chhabra1@gmail.com
Pradeep@pradeepchhabra.com
@pradeep_chhabra,
https://in.linkedin.com/in/pradeepchhabra,
https://www.facebook.com/pradeep.chhabra.77

Preface

Ideas for writing this book subsequent to my earlier book UNCORK YOURSELF NOT BOTTLES emerged post the reactions to the book which were in plenty and were very encouraging for me. Feedback came from all age groups through LinkedIn, Tweets and FB and by word of mouth. Encouragement from the extended family was overwhelming. All my worries of being first time author were ill founded. My conviction of trying to be first time right also got fortified.

This book covers topics that stay relevant irrespective of the changes in technology, environment, social, political economic, financial, local and global landscape.

Topics are relevant whether you are an Engineer, Chartered accountant, Doctor, Architect, Journalist, Lawyer, Media person, Sports lover, Critic or any other function so long as you are working with people around you who can be your spouse, colleagues, peers, boss, customer, patient, friend subordinate, attendant, driver or any other We are all in the business of managing people. Everyone needs to improve one's respective ability to deal with people.

You can't live in isolation and should therefore be always conscious of the fact of what you speak and how you speak, you dress, you walk ,your body language expresses the words you speak how you write your mails or WhatsApp, your way of smiling (fake or genuine), listening to others, addressing and treating persons below you who are powerless and are in the lower strata of the society, your behaviour when no one is watching you, what you are reading if at all you do, your choice of words, vocabulary, and your dominant use of few selected words defines you all.

This book covers issues relevant to your Professional life. Be aware of your deeds irrespective of your level. Remain as if you were on day one of your career on your enthusiasm, learning and efforts to succeed. Be agile or you will be run over sooner than later. Be ready to accept your area of weakness and once you do that you are on your path to the next orbit and many higher orbits thereafter. Be ready to communicate in a manner that you can figure out as to what is perceived and not what is spoken.

In professional life and in long careers there are always times when you need the Company to support you and vice versa, situation of Company needing your support will also come. Be ready for these situations. I personally have gone through very difficult times in my personal life and support provided by my employer was exceptional.

Are you conscious of your happiness, humility Index like other personal indices of Approachability, Likability, Listening, Luck, Trust and Simplicity as explained in my earlier book? Do you love status quo in your personal and professional life? Figure it out. Maintaining status quo is the most dangerous attribute both personally and professionally.

Post few successes or after occupying a strategic and important position in professional life, have you reached a stage of intellectual arrogance when you have a feeling that you can do no wrong? Check it out. You may have already started hurting yourself.

Are you aware as to how long your present job is going to last? Are you employed or employable? Are you in your comfort zone with current job? Are you doing the same thing year after year resulting in one-year experience multiple times?

Find ways to smile, find ways to feel and stay young mentally as you grow older and one sure way of doing this is to spend time with your school and college friends. Believe me if you are not spending time with your friends of yesteryears, you are growing older at a speed faster than expected.

Book is in two parts, first part is before and second after the interval as interval is the midpoint of your career when you are set up as a professional, raring to touch the top. Don't you wish to be Lion and not a Mouse, don't you wish to be a Butterfly and not an Ant in Corporate circus? Let us begin…...

Pradeep Chhabra

Contents

The human brain has 100 billion neurons, each neuron is connected to 10 thousand other neurons; Sitting on your shoulders is the most complicated object in the known universe. — Michio Kaku

Your Personal Operating System (PoS)

When did you last update it?

henever I go to the settings of my iPhone and look at software update, it smartly says your software is updated and specifies a number, presently 12.1.2 (As on Dec 2018), iPhone was launched in 2007 and till today we have had 95 plus upgrades with an average of say 9-10 upgrades every year. After every few days, operating system of your iPhone is upgraded for one function or the other, making our life easier and smoother. Similar upgrades happen in other operating systems all over in any gadget or application. Upgrades have reached a level that computers now ask humans very often to prove that they are not robots.

Let's talk about our very personal and our own and self-developed operating system in our head, our mind which is the best computer system. Let's call your brain as the hardware and mind as your software. Brain is the outer shell which is tough and protects all soft things inside like any cell phone. You cannot do anything with the size, shape and appearance of the outer shell i.e. your brain, but mind is one thing which determines everything in your life. You are the owner, and the CEO with full control over what goes in and what comes out. While many things can go in depending upon the environment, circumstances, status and position you are in, what matters is what comes out. All businesses make money with value addition on inputs. How much value addition you are doing? Inputs are available for free or whatever you decide that must go in. Just Google or Bing and any information in the world will be at your command and can get inside you in a jiffy. What you make out of this stuff and what use you put this into will define you in the long run. Like your iPhone or any other phone like Google plus operating on Android, there are multiple Apps (Applications you have personally installed in your mind). Some of us can quickly do maths calculations, some can figure out any spelling or grammar mistakes, some of you know all historical facts, some of us are good at remembering the names and the list goes on and on.

It's specific to each human being. Everyone has its own version. Everyone has its own distinct and patented operating system. These individual systems over a period have become so hardened and the internal wires have intertwined in such a rigid manner that this operating system takes a lot of effort and time to upgrade. In a way, you have developed your own neural highways in your mind with the experiences of your life. Each of the neural highways in your mind has its own toll plazas acting as a barrier for you. In certain cases, individual's personal operating system comprising of all the network of highways and toll plazas cannot be upgraded at all as the owner has locked it up with a password that is not even known to him. In some other cases, sole owner of the personal operating system refuses to upgrade and feels good doing the same thing same way year after year but expects to get different and at times spectacular results. This personal operating system determines how fast and how long you are going to take to reach your defined goals in life.

Your operating system has full control on how you think, how you use the words for articulating your thoughts which become your actions, deeds, habits and consequently your destiny. We need to evolve our personal operating system continuously till we are on this planet. You can't assume a position that your operating system has reached the optimum level, and nothing can be done further to upgrade this. Lots of managers reach that position before the interval (Discussed in detail in a later chapter) and then stagnation in life starts. There are endless things you can do to fix bugs in your personal operating system starting from:

- What time you talk to yourself every day?
- Have you kept a time slot for visiting mental gym?
- Communication skill.
- Dressing sense.
- Networking ability.
- Happiness index.
- Likability, luck, listening, approachability Index.
- Are you low on financial security and stability, are you fragile financially?
- Are you in the right company within the company you work for?
- Are you in a position to manage your boss?
- Are you low on your social skills?
- How do you assess and rate your Emotional Quotient?

Each human being has lots of deficiencies and none of us is perfect. Habits, (which become road blocks in your progress) get formed over a period and changing them needs some raw courage and determination to change. It's possible in case you wish to. We all need to strive hard to step on to next operating level. Chances of your getting outdated, obsolete and becoming a bonsai increase rapidly in case you are not upgrading your operating system on regular basis. How about fixing one bug every month or in a quarter and releasing Version 2.0, 3.0 and thereon of your personal operating system. At times you may have to format few of the segments of the system and start all over again.

Which one bug you want to fix first and which one afterwards is purely your personal priority. First important point is that you must identify the bugs first. Some of your best friends, family members can certainly help you in identifying the bugs provided you have the intent to receive feedback with open eyes and ears.

So, go ahead and fix bugs in your personal operating system as early as possible and be as updated as your gadgets. Be in control of your mind and not let your mind control you. You are the pilot, you need to navigate, let it not be on auto pilot. You are the boss and you know where you are going?

Release your upgraded version every month, every quarter or as soon as you deem fit.

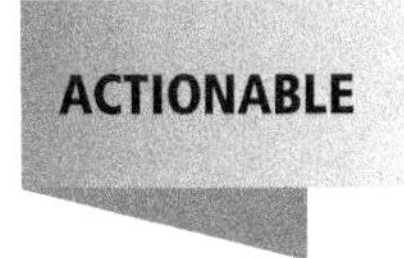

**Identify bugs in your POS
and fix them**

Wanting to be someone else is a waste of the person you are!
—Kurt Cobain

2

Always Seek Professional Advice!

You should know who knows what, you need not know everything!

My house lift was tripping regularly and repeatedly after few hours of operation. It is under regular maintenance contract by a reputed supplier. Maintenance team was put into action and it concluded that all is well with lift and I need to replace MCB (Miniature circuit breaker) as it is faulty and is tripping. MCB is the input point from where current flows to the lift to operate. MCB is outside the scope of maintenance team of the lift. Revised specification of MCB with higher amps was handed over to me for further action. Complaint was closed for action on customer side by the maintenance team. I was not satisfied but had to agree with them as they put everything in black and white.

Emergency call was made to a senior professional electrician who came rushing He asks for a broom, cleans the MCB and says: You will not have to call me again for this. It is working since. It is few months now. Some of the lessons which remained with me in professional life and were fortified again with this example make lots of sense in our day to day work & personal life.

- ▶ Never interfere in other's work, leave aside even suggesting.
- ▶ Always look for best professional advice.

There will be many such cases or issues in professional life when things keep going around with no solution. It is a fact that person who knows will stick his neck out and resolve the matter in no time; others will take you on a long and indecisive route, making things complex and time consuming. Always look out for the person who knows, you do not have to know everything, you only need to know who knows what. Your competence lies in assessing and figuring out who is the most competent person for the job and make him and facilitate him to finish the task.

It is a fact of life that a person who knows the solution to a problem will have all the time under the sun and on the contrary all those persons who have no clue or no answer will have no time to resolve the problem. Never ever approach a person again who says that he has no time for helping you out to solve a specific problem, most of the time he has no idea or no solution to offer and you have approached the wrong person. This includes all those people in our personal and professional network who also take a position saying come later or remind me after some days. It borders on arrogance and needs to be dealt suitably.

Be vigilant in identifying and using the skill sets of people around you.

Success is nothing more than a few simple disciplines, practised every day.
—Jim Rohn

3

Discover Your X Factor

What are you good at?

Do you speak and write well and, therefore, communicate well? Do you dress well? Do you behave well? Do you sing well? Do you run well and can complete a marathon? Which games indoor or outdoor you are good at? Do you dance well? Do you act or posture well? Is your sense of humour way ahead of others? Do you play an instrument well? Do you cook well? Do you write a good poetry or a dialogue? Are you good at networking? Are you good at teaching?

Your X factor is what you are good at or what are you passionate about. What comes very naturally to you without any effort? Where you don't feel burdened or bothered to do and will take no time in doing it if you are given an opportunity?

Every human being is good at something or the other which needs to be discovered. At times this discovery takes place at very early stage to himself or by his colleagues, friends, parents or say neighbours. Once discovered early, practised, rehearsed, polished and presented with good confidence can change the course of your life.

Have you ever tried to figure out what are you good at? Listen carefully to your friends, peers and colleagues as to which area you get complimented the most. These things get conveyed in the heat of the moment at a given time and you need to reflect upon them when you are alone or on your pillow. Develop a work plan to strengthen that area. Can that be taken to a higher professional level which can take the course of your life?

Film star and actor Sushant Singh left his engineering college education from DTU (Delhi Technical University) mid-way after completing three years and has since had a successful career in films. He discovered his X factor in the middle of his education. There will be many such instances. One of my class mates, (Mechanical engineering) confided after four decades of leaving college that his X factor was in architectural domain which he could not pursue after schooling for whatever reason and seriously regrets not having done so. His ability to visualise in domain of architectural segments remains exceptional. He helps lots of people in doing what is needed for upgrading their abodes.

As a business leader, it's your ability to discover the X factors of others and if you can do it consistently year after year, be assured that you will have a formidable team with rich talent. Dividends that will accrue to you as a leader will be disproportionately high to the efforts you may have put in. Everyone will want to get into your team. Mahendra Singh Dhoni, former Indian captain of Indian cricket team has exceptional capability of discovering X factor of his team mates. He knows who is needed and at what time.

Famous and talented Hindi film actor Manoj Bajpayee confirms to have discovered his X factor at the age of four.

A poor team leader will start developing the X factor of his team mates which do not exist. His team goes down the drain with poor results. In all seriousness do convey if you spot the X factor of your team mates, friends, or peers to them. At times this discovery takes lots of time. Earlier you discover better it is.

"You can achieve your dreams with your X factor! Figure out your X factor as early as you can.

Your brand is what other people say about you
when you're not in the room
—Jeff Bezos

Your Personal Reputation
Nothing is more valuable

Nothing is more valuable than your personal reputation on multiple fronts which gets tested day in day out. This is applicable during all stages of your career from the day you step in to the last day of your work till you hang up your boots. Your personal reputation if acceptable to people who matter can accelerate your career growth, otherwise very soon you will be found in some remote corner of the organization without a meaningful role. You will be left behind, and the impact will be visible by few years of difference between you and your peers or batch mates. It has been seen that many careers get destroyed by a sullied personal reputation. It has been seen to have happened to real intelligent and go getter professionals after the interval as described in a later chapter.

Take good care of what you do on daily basis. Everyone is noticed, everyone is observed, and the good or bad points of yours are generally discussed in the personal and private dialogues of your team members, department and the people who matter.

What is written in your appraisal note comes later than this dossier of yours. An exceptional performance in a year but few blots on personal integrity, or general level of conduct being below than expected standard will not let you pass the gate for next level. Keep your personal reputation above everything, with no compromise on any of the laid down standards, conventions or acceptable practices of your company. Let this be your way of living in your official life from day one to last day.

Change of company or job at times leads to say less stringent expectations in the new environment. Stick to your way of keeping your reputation above board. Few of the important points which make or mar your reputation in the official and personal networks are laid below:

- ► Ability to stick to the time schedule be it your daily attendance, or presence in meetings or elsewhere for important events including parties for fun. Persons with no respect for time are generally not a respected lot. (Exceptional cases of delay are well understood by everyone).Some of the toxic guys consider it improper to be on time and consider it below their dignity.

- ► Language both verbal and written you use while communicating. Is it I or We dominated? Are you using impolite words which can shake up the mental balance of other persons?

- ► Your body gestures while dealing with subordinate and supporting staff.

- ► Your attitude towards the women in general.

- ► Do people trust you on face value with all the seriousness or whatever you say is discounted by few percentage points?

- ► Are you consistent in your approach over matters of individuals?

- ► Your personal priorities, team priorities and companies' priorities are in which order. If they are as indicated here, you will not travel far and will not last long in a role. Always have it in the order of company first, team second and you at last.

- ► Do you raise the bar for performance each time a goal is achieved, thereby challenging people to perform?

- ► Do you provide freedom and space to juniors to act and perform?

- ▶ Do you let go a person without any reprimand who has committed a genuine error of judgement or mistake?
- ▶ Do you deliver what you commit?
- ▶ Do you fudge your travel bills, work timings while away?
- ▶ Do you encourage your juniors or team mates to do improper acts of conduct within team or teams or seniors in other departments?
- ▶ Are you candid in your approach?
- ▶ How do you conduct yourself in a social get together say after drinks or otherwise?

ACTIONABLE　　**Develop your personal SOPs (Standard operating procedures) which others envy and emulate!**

The world doesn't celebrate your similarity
but your difference"
— Bernard Kelvin Clive

Develop Back Bone

Stand out

*I*T's a sure way to stand out of the crowd. Developing back bone is your ability to say something ahead of others which others may be just thinking. It's your ability to stand up against an argument when everyone is nodding its head in affirmation. It's your ability to come out with an offer which the customer cannot refuse. It's your ability to decide things ahead of others. It's your ability to stick your neck out when there is no one who has the guts to do.

Just to quote an example from the life of Mahendra Singh Dhoni (MSD), former Indian cricket captain, while playing the cricket World Cup finals in 2011, against Sri Lanka in Mumbai, he advanced his position ahead of few other regular positions where others play. Most unusual thing to happen especially when stakes are high. This was the critical moment of the game and odds of winning or losing were balanced for both the teams. Everyone was surprised. This was an ample demonstration of his courage of conviction. No one told him to do so, it was his judgement and he went over to the coach and conveyed him his plan. He didn't consult any one nor did he seek permission from any one. With full responsibility on his shoulders he went on to win the match and hit a winning six. That's what defines your ability to achieve something great in life. You need to stand up and stand out. The results can go both ways, you can be on the mat or you would be holding the cup, but if you do not try you won't succeed either. Laurels and appreciation were showered on MSD, and whole nation was in indulgence and he truly deserved it.

Another example of back bone to achieve something in life is of Sri Lankan cricketer and former captain Marvan Attapatu who was dropped few times from the team as he scored duck on each occasion. It was possibly after three come backs when he secured his place in the team and then went on to lead his country. It is only back bone which drives you.

You need to be aware of the circumstances in day to day working to be able to take a bold stand on the work or policy or any other issue which is under deliberation at a given moment. You should be able to access information ahead of others. Your ability to foresee and anticipate events, crisis or any development ahead of others will help you in building your back bone. Your ability to make other people see your view point irrespective of the rank of the person you are putting across your point will make the difference. You need to prepare well in advance ahead of the event and discuss with yourself as to what are the possibilities of your intervention.

Back bone gets developed as you work, provided you are willing to admit a mistake if it has occurred and rectify the same with all earnestness. One who works makes mistakes. Mistake can be of judgement or assumptions or can be a plain error in calculations leading to poor forecast of demand. In routine operational jobs, mistakes are a part of life. Just yesterday a courier company who was engaged in book distribution was checking up with all the customers whether right book has been delivered as there was some goof up at the packing end which resulted in large number of wrong deliveries. Imagine the pain and cost of recollecting and redistributing all the parcels within the city and the anguish of the customers. This mistake once done will be a lesson for life so that it does not happen again. All engaged persons will be cautious on every step. Leadership here went into a war mode by:

- ► Managing the situation in quickest possible time.
- ► Fix up the loose ends as to why it happened.
- ► Counsel the persons involved.

Many companies show the guts of advertising that theirs is the best price and if you get a better price, take the refund. That is a real confident statement to make and it shows the aggression in decision making and showing to the entire segment of the customers. These are the simple examples of routine nature where confidence was shown in managing a situation gone wrong and in demonstrating a courageous sales instance.

Developing back bone will make you stand apart and pay rich dividends. Make this a habit. It is possible. Benefits that will accrue will be immense and disproportionately high to the efforts you put in. Opportunities arise very often to demonstrate that you have the backbone to survive, thrive and leapfrog to the next level of professional excellence.

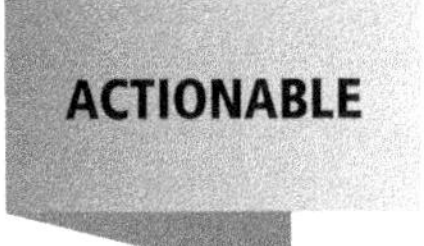

Develop ability to foresee consequences of your actions, way to develop backbone!

"Handle them carefully,
for words have more power than atom bombs"
—Pearl Strachan Hurd

6

Choose the Right Words

*An injury caused by tongue takes the
longest time to heal!*

First of all ask yourself at the outset as to why are you opening your mouth? Is the purpose of what you are about to say or what people want you to say or they want to hear or talk about is known to you or it is just an unwanted reaction to someone's speech?

To be politically correct at times you need to say only what someone wants to hear, and on other occasions you need to speak what is to be said and not what audience wants to hear. Therefore, understanding of the situation, you are in or you are presented with is very relevant to your selection of words before you open your mouth.

Be aware of the time frame in which audience wants you to deliver your message. Few seconds here and there will not make much difference, but too much of difference in the time you take and what is allotted to you will spoil the fun and the schedule of the program. Attention span of the audience is generally very limited, and people get disconnected quickly.

Professional life requires you to articulate your thoughts before speaking in various forums, be it is in one to one meeting with your boss, while giving feed back to your subordinates or say your team meeting or giving a presentation to large number of persons in a seminar. While generally we prepare ahead of time on what to speak, but the experience shows that we all fumble at the critical moment of conversation when a counter argument is to be made or a final punch line which should be the closing point to be made.

Notice the flawless extempore speeches made by Barack Obama, former President of USA with appropriate words, and right kind of emphasis, pauses and body language in perfect sync. Years of hard work and practice in loneliness have gone into this performance of his which he delivers repeatedly in various forums. Long hours of preparation are needed to give a perfect speech of few minutes.

We all think faster than we speak. We all think in our own ways and in our own languages and then this gets converted into the spoken words. Part of our emotions also pushes us to choose some critical words which can turn the discussions in different directions. Subsequent discussions get focused on what you said or what you meant or what you intended to say. So be aware that you need to find the right words for each occasion for articulating your thoughts in a manner so that it reflects what you intend to say and is not misinterpreted or misrepresented.

Do take into consideration the background of the persons you are speaking to. It may be a good idea to use slang words with young team in an informal chat, say after office hours. It may not be appropriate to use same words in a formal chat with the same team on a topic of serious discussions to set targets and goals.

Level of understanding, education, experience and background of the person to whom you are speaking should go into consideration while selecting words. Challenge always lies in not what you have said, but what is perceived by the person of what you have said. On more than few occasions, there is variance between what was spoken and what was understood or taken away from the meeting. Audience also looks into how you are saying besides what you are saying. Is your body stance arrogance or humble?

It's always good to pause, think and speak rather than just blabbering on whatever comes to your mind while doing conversation on topics which matter to both the parties, be it negotiation or just an introduction meeting or setting the agenda for task ahead. There were always long pauses in the speeches of Late Atal Bihari Vajpayee, former Prime Minister of India, who was a speaker of a very high level & standard and loved by masses.

Right words do not come naturally to most of us, therefore consider allocating some time to, chose, rehearse, recall, and remember the words for appropriate moment. All experienced professionals anticipate the events when they will be called to speak which can be few minutes away at times and they do a mental run of what to speak even when others are speaking.

In crucial conversation, repeating few words multiple times brings the emphasis and clarity on your statements. Some of the outstanding spoken words which come instantly from a person are remembered for life time.

Be brief and to the point, judge the body reactions of listeners and carry on with what you need to say. An injury caused by tongue takes the longest time to heal therefore; selection of words is the most critical aspect to your likability index.

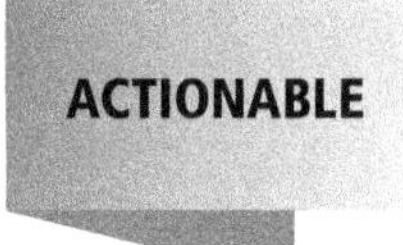

Read as much as you can, there is always a better word. Always look up for the meaning in case of doubt!

"It usually takes me more than three weeks to prepare a good impromptu speech"
—Mark Twain

Make it Extempore

True cutting edge in life

Very often in professional life, you are expected to speak either in meetings or in a gathering of large people on the subject that is known to you. While you will do all the preparation for speaking on the subject by way of points made from all aspects. Please note that in case you get up to speak from a paper, your impact would be half of what your expectation is. Speaking from a paper without eye contact with the audience would make even a wonderful presentation look mediocre or below par.

Moment people see that you are going to rely on some paper to speak on the subject, most of the audience will get disconnected and look other way under the impression that somebody has written the speech and you are just here to read it without any contribution to the topic or the subject. Your impact on the audience will be minimal and in fact they will eagerly wait for you to finish your speech as early as possible.

It takes a lot of hard work, preparation and rehearsal to make a speech without referring to any papers and once you succeed in doing so you will be remembered for very long time to come. You can always keep a paper for ready reference via bullet points to prompt you to deliver the speech in a structured manner and it appeals to the audience. Howsoever hard it may be, give a try, delivery by way of extempore speech will fetch you instant recognition and fame over a period of time. Expectation from you for all times to come would be to beat your own standards. People would love listening to you.

As seen often, people at very senior-level just go through the motions of giving a speech by reading the paper. I recall that a very senior person was to give speech at both times, welcoming the participants and thanking them at the end of the proceedings. Both the drafts were given to him ahead of time and proceedings to begin. It so happened that he started reading thanks note at the beginning of the proceedings instead of welcome speech and realized that well after he had read a para and then he realized what he was doing was wrong much to the amusement of the gathering. All the team members were embarrassed to the hilt at this act of their leader who was a very senior person. This is what happens when somebody else is working for you and you take it for granted that you have to just stand up and read and not deliver what is required to be told to the audience.

All smart and competent professionals speak extempore. It needs burning mid night oil, it requires practice, it requires you to speak in loneliness multiple times same thing again and again to deliver a perfect speech.

This habit if formed in early stages of your career will make so much difference throughout your life that you will be asked to hold the mike on more than one occasion which itself will give a boost to your career. Another point of significance is selection of right and critical words which impact the mind. Use of simple and easily understood words make the difference. An extempore speech or a talk of five minutes is good enough to beat a written speech of double the time. Learn to do this early in life.

ACTIONABLE **Practise in loneliness to speak without a paper. Record, Listen, Repeat, and Record again.**

*Learning about and from your customers
is not always easy and needs commitment
to continual observation*

—John Rampton

Power of Observation

Your gateway to superhighway of success

While in college, it's all about the grades, be it in written exam or viva. It's all about individual performance within set agenda or course which is known. The only surprise element is whether you get those questions to answer which you know very well or have worked on or you get those whom you thought were not relevant and may not come in the exams. Your performance therefore is subject to hard work and bit of luck on the day of exam. Assuming you do very well and score the top marks, you are on the high and walk with pride in college corridors. You will be remembered for life time as a topper by your batch mates. Its 42 years since I left the college but in our private conversation with college friends a topper remains a topper, irrespective of his progress or status in professional life.

Welcome to new world of corporate life. No sooner you enter the corporate world all habits or traits acquired in academic world will not serve any purpose. There won't be any homework or questions for which answers need to be prepared.

Here things are ambiguous on many fronts. Here there are many answers to the same question and all of them may be correct. Here you need to observe many things and figure out for yourself as to

- ► How People communicate with each other. Is it a formal mail, or is it word of mouth, WhatsApp, face to face, or one to one or in meetings?

- ► How do you arrange a meeting? Do you just go over and tell people? How much notice is needed?

- ► How do you meet seniors, is it just knock the door and get in or seek appointment?

- ► Is sitting late in the office the most important aspect, whether work or no work?

- ► Is PPT the most preferred way to discuss or a word document is good enough?

- ► Is candour encouraged in official meetings or you need to be politically correct all the time, even if it means that you are not communicating what you should be, but what people like?

- ► Is a week end strict no for any official matters or people do exchange mails?

- ► What is the dress code for office and parties?

- ► Travel protocols with your team, boss or customers.

- ► Where do you make calls from in case of long telecons or conference calls (Go out in a room or you sit in your work place and have it with earphones ?

- ► Is eating allowed on your work station?

- ► Is Customer the boss or your hierarchical boss is the supremo? Be aware all successful companies are so customer centric that hierarchical boss is a step below.

- ► What's the code of conduct in town hall meetings?

- ► What's the tolerance for time discipline?

List is endless and more you observe, adopt and follow, your acceptance level goes up. Your likability index will be very high like getting A + in school or college. First few days the challenge is to increase your likability index in the system by adapting to the prevalent culture.

This phenomenon of observation is valid when you change your company or job or department in the same company. Each new job or even transfer within a company will throw up these challenges which are not major issues but impact your likability index. Be aware of these parameters.

In corporate life, change of boss or Head of business or function can change things overnight. Be aware that new boss's priorities become your priority and earlier you change course and direction, happy you will be. All this comes only if you have sharp power of observation. Earlier you adopt this habit of observation; your path to success will open up as a super highway

ACTIONABLE   **Observe people silently
with a smile. Draw lessons!**

Commitment is binary. You are either 100% committed or not at all. All partial and conditional commitments fall in the latter category.

—Amir Ghannad

Power of Commitment

Takes your brand value to next level!

*I*n our daily life, be at home or in office quite often we are required to commit. Commitment can be of time, money, some assistance in academics, some assistance at professional front, just a telephone call at a given time, bringing few things back home in return, plan for holidays, attending a party and many such other things impacting day to day life of yours and other members in family or the peer group in office or the boss. Most of the personal commitments to family, friends and parents generally are given less priority than official commitments for sake of job and professional progress.

Over a period, family generally reduces dependence on you on the plea that you are a busy person and need not be bothered for any help. Fact of the matter is that it's an attitude issue. If you have a mental makeup of assisting and helping others, you would generally not refuse to help and will give a commitment to do the job within the expected timeframe. This habit of making a commitment first and then delivering in time repeatedly for family, friends leads to a solid attitude of adherence to the task on the professional front. You would first keep a note of all the commitments and then one by one meet all of them without any reminders.

No follow up is needed and everyone around you has the confidence that whatever is committed will be delivered. It may on occasions take a little more time than anticipated. Have seen people saying for persons with attitude of commitment that if you have told him, take it as done. It's just a matter of time. If he has promised a call back, it will come.

Be aware that your attitude on personal front will get superimposed or replicated on professional front as well and in the long run what habits you have in family circles will be visible on professional circles as well. Mind you if you are stickler for time in office, same thing will get replicated at home as well. Be evasive at home on making commitments, unknowingly the habit will emerge in office as well. You are the same person and will not be able to demonstrate or act differently at home or at office.

Recall few years back in an annual business review meeting when a detailed presentation was being made by a senior person who was the business leader in a large conference room of more than 40 persons. Person chairing the meeting was the Chairman of the organization. Chairman had some observations and plans which he put across the team for implementation. He was expecting some questions or discussions by the participants as to how and why of it. He was expecting some concerns as the proposed plan was different and never tried earlier anywhere in the organization. Plan was full of challenges for the team. All that did not happen.

Moment he finished, senior person who was the business leader giving presentation mentioned with all the confidence at his command TAKE IT AS DONE AND YOU WILL HAVE THE CONFIRMATION TO THIS EFFECT ON YOUR TABLE BEFORE CLOSE OF BUSINESS ON A SPECIFIED DATE, WHICH WAS MUCH EARLIER THAN ANY ONE'S EXPECTATION. There was a pin drop silence in the hall. It was a delight to see the expression on the face of the Chairman. That's the power of commitment. You can make people speechless, eliminate the time spent on discussions, increase your brand equity, and challenge your team to perform at next level

ACTIONABLE　　**Develop courage to commit.
You will leapfrog to next orbit!**

Good manners will open doors that
the best education cannot.
—Clarence Thomas —Amir Ghannad

10

Power of Etiquette

More powerful than any other skill!

Etiquettes of right kind which are appropriate for the occasion will make lots of difference to your career and will give a booster shot every now and then. It is a sure fast forward catalyst. It will compensate you for all your inadequacies on other skills. Lack of etiquette can destroy the career of an otherwise intelligent and accomplished person on many other fronts. We are referring to a good behaviour, acceptable behaviour as per existing conventions and practices prevalent around. Few simple things matter a lot.

There are lots of dos and don'ts which you need to observe, assimilate and conduct yourself in a manner that whatever you do is liked by the people. Some of the issues which border on bad manners and will make you stand out on unacceptable behaviour are:

- Not waiting patiently in the queue while waiting for the lift to arrive as you reach office or at any other place like airport, hotel or for a place of client meeting.
- Not greeting persons around with a smile or a gesture appropriate for the time.
- Receiving the guests or the business associates without getting up from your seat.
- Not offering a seat to a senior person who is made to stand for a while in a meeting.
- Poor table manners like talking with your mouth full, not leaving the stuff served for others.

- ▶ Arriving late for the meeting, where you are the host and making guests wait.
- ▶ Occupying a place meant for others who are more important.
- ▶ Dressing inappropriately for a meeting where a dress code is the advisory.
- ▶ Always in a critical and negative mood or mode.
- ▶ Attending meeting while chewing a gum or any other substance.
- ▶ Not finishing your speech in time.
- ▶ Not carrying the relevant data for the discussion agenda.
- ▶ Not introducing persons to others who are not known to each other.
- ▶ Not sharing the relevant details in time for the occasion to the persons who should know.
- ▶ Talking loudly on mobile either in a meeting or at a public place.
- ▶ Rude behaviour with subordinate staff in office or with service personnel in a party or in a hotel.

While this list can go on and on, ensure that your personal and professional behaviour is at par with minimum acceptable standards of that area or the profession or the position you are in. Good etiquettes will not only fast forward your career, make your team perform and deliver results, establish your personal brand, make you approachable and lovable person but will also make you the first choice to be in any team.

Bad behaviour will generally close all doors for you from all the emerging opportunities on the horizon, slow down your pace, isolate you from real good people who matter. Your network will shrink faster than you can imagine. You will not be invited for the important meetings. You will be the last person to receive information relevant and critical to you

I have seen persons with not so good skill sets on many other fronts but with top class etiquettes leaving many other far more competent, capable, knowledgeable persons behind in the corporate ladder.

You need to be observant in figuring out what is proper and good behaviour from the people around you. They will stand out and look different. Notice the small things about them and start practising day in day out. You will need lots of practice till it gets so deeply ingrained in your system that a good behaviour is a synonym of your personal brand. After some time with regular practice it will come out so naturally from you as if you were born with this kind of behaviour. Few things amongst many other are listed below:

- Treating all with equal respect irrespective of the level you are at.
- Your body language is full of grace and politeness.
- Talking with eye contact. Remembering names of individuals whom you do not meet so regularly.
- Holding crucial conversation with all candour and appropriate use of words.
- Dressed in an elegant manner appropriate for the occasion.
- As a host ensuring all guests are comfortable and are given due attention.
- As a guest, be courteous to other co guests and express good words for the host.
- Be professional on time commitments for all meetings or functions where you are the host or invitee.
- Criticism or disapproval is conveyed in a manner that is perceived as a valuable input.
- Giving a smile very often to bring a very positive atmosphere
- Encouraging and appreciating others whenever needed.
- Not letting anyone criticize a person who is not present in the meeting.
- Saying thank you or sorry as often as needed.

As mentioned, list is endless; keep observing and practising you will only improve on daily basis. Remember your excellent technical skills can go down the drain if you lack in proper etiquettes to use them in person, in a meeting or in large get-to-gethers, People will remember how you are saying and not what you are saying. People will remember your expressions and not your words. People will remember for life time if you hurt them without any reason.

ACTIONABLE   **Imbibe good etiquettes for all occasions!**

The people who cast the votes do not decide an election, the people who count the votes do.
—Joseph Stalin

Who Decides?

Locate the Hero?

$\mathcal{I}$t is really a challenge to figure out as to who decides on a certain proposal in a company. In large companies, it's generally well defined who is the final signatory to say go ahead. Interesting part is he, the final signatory, cannot say yes on sighting of the proposal, even if it means a good amount in savings or increase in realizations. Proposals are vetted by many in the hierarchy before a go ahead or green signal is given.

Challenge here is where to start to market your proposal. One must go through many stages repeatedly to present the same proposal. But someone in the hierarchy will carry more weight than many others and here lies the trick of finding this person. He will make your proposal move faster in the system. He will be the guy who will own it and defend before the person(s) who are expected to say final yes.

Challenge is to locate this gentleman (Let's call him Hero) and provide him with all the ammunition to fight your battle. In most of the cases where proposal do not get the approval, Hero is not located or is absent in the system. Please appreciate you cannot meet the final signatory all the time but our Hero is approachable and can be reached any time on phone, mail, WhatsApp, Messenger and will provide you updates as to where is the proposal and what are the obstacles in the system.

Hero is a man with full professional integrity and is not the middleman who helps or eases any deals. Hero is the person here who knows the subject and is willing to undergo the challenge and experience of making both the sides say yes. Hero is the person who sees the value in the proposition and has full courage of his personal conviction on the merits of the proposal.

Now how do you find the Hero? Here lies the challenge. Few visits to solicit business and discussions thereof, Hero will emerge on its own and you will be able to spot him clearly. He will be the person who will be asking the most difficult questions. Hero may not be in the senior segment of the hierarchy. He is the person who wants to impress his bosses and can analyse and present the proposal with full confidence as to what is being decided.

In smaller set ups it is easier and faster to figure out who decides. Here again it may not be the top man. In corporate world authorities of persons at the top are used by smart persons who may be lower down the hierarchy. These are the smart guys and are the real leaders. Approaching top man all the time and expecting results may not yield any result. Top man also needs a sounding board.

**Spot the right person
in the hierarchy!**

Turn data into information and information into insight
—Carly Fiorina

12

Market Intelligence

Sure way to grow personally and professionally

*I*rrespective of the job you are in or position you are at, life is all about growth. Its personal growth as well as the growth of business that matters. You can't grow if your business does not grow. Is your business growing at a rate which is ahead of competition? If your business is growing at a rate which is more than rate of growth of entire industry then you are in the driver's seat. You deserve to be congratulated and if yours is a public held company listed in stock exchanges, stake holders would love your company and pay a higher premium for your stock. No business can survive without market intelligence on product, price, promotion, cost, quality, service, logistics and trust factor of the company and persons handling the transactions.

Getting marketing intelligence is literally getting market place to office. Rely on person in the last place in the hierarchy who is really sweating it out day in day out. Give him the freedom and space; encourage him to speak with candour. You will be appalled to know what is perceived at 30000 feet in headquarters is far away from what's happening on the ground. Policy making can be skewed and unproductive if made without involvement of front-line officers. Who would know better as to what a small car buyer wants, obviously the front-line sales person and not the smart dude sitting before the laptop at headquarters. Smart dude will be smarter if he spends considerable time with the sales man hearing from them rather than talking to them. More often it happens the other way.

In yet another example, delivery boy at a fuel retail outlet knows by mere sight of the motorist whether he is a tank full customer or customer who will buy with monetary value of say 100 or 200 bucks. Many customers buy fuel by monetary consideration and not volume consideration irrespective of the fuel price.

Getting market intelligence is everyone's job across the hierarchy and across the functions. It is an everyday function. It is every one's function whether you are a marketing, operations, accounting, human resource or a logistics functionary. Contribution to Market intelligence needs to be done by all from front line officers to CEO. Quality of inputs will vary as everyone has its own circle of interaction.

Recall that a CEO of a beverage company in a key note address on the subject saying very proudly that he travels once a week in a delivery truck in hot weather to get to ground realties. Hot weather was mentioned specifically as beverage sales are at their peak at that time. That's the right way to capture as to what is happening where customer comes and opens his wallet.

If you can bring knowledge about competition from the market place to the table which adds value to your business, it means a lot and you will be respected in your work domain. Gathering market intelligence and developing this as a habit from early stages of your career will certainly take you to new heights.

Market intelligence is needed even if your product is doing very well. It's always important to analyse the success, failures get analysed in any case. If you or your product is successful, sit back and figure it out. Build on these strengths as someone somewhere would be quickly copying all that you have done to catch up with you.

How do you get the meaningful & useful information? Visit the websites, retail outlets, stores of various competitors. Go through published material of the competition in the public domain. Talk to their customers in a listening mode. Read their balance sheet,

Director's statement, hold may be one share only to get the invite to their Annual General meetings. Follow them on LinkedIn, FB and other social sites. Get invited to their sponsored public functions, meet them in industry events. Opportunities to get the meaningful information about competition are quite a few, one only needs to have the bent of mind, application, effort and acceptance in mind that it is critical to the business you are engaged in.

In today's fast changing world, companies not having an eye on market intelligence can get literally out of business in no time. Recall the rapid downfall of Nokia hand phone manufacturer for not noticing the changes in market place at first and then not acting upon it. At a given time, they were holding market share in access of 75% in the segment of top 10 models in the industry. Customers were buying Nokia as their first preference. Nokia management continued to ignore all market signals for a considerable time before it became too late for them to retrieve the situation.

Mobile market is now on two systems Android and IOS. Symbian the operating system of Nokia is nowhere around. Nokia failed to read the market signals that mobile market was moving from hardware to software dominance. Competitors like Samsung and Apple were getting their Apps outsourced and moving ahead at a rapid pace.

Let's move out from office and spend considerable time away from work stations or cabins. Consider getting market intelligence as daily dose of essential elements for good health of yours professionally and of your business.

Sumant Moolgaokar (5 March 1906 – 1989) was an Indian industrialist, known as architect of Tata Motors. He also remained Vice-Chairman of Tata Steel. He was awarded the Padma Bhushan, third-highest civilian honour by the Government of India in 1990. He would vanish in lunch hour while in Tata Motors to the bewilderment of everyone and appear back in office before close of lunch hour. On daily basis for a long time he was doing this much to the surprise of all colleagues. Lots of speculation was going on in the office on his possible rendezvous. After few days someone tracked him down to a Dhaba (way side eatery) and found him sitting amongst truck drivers seeking feedback from his users. There cannot be a better way of getting Market Intelligence straight from the user in the language they speak and is easy to communicate by customer.

Best place to get the Market Intelligence is to be at the point where ultimate customer comes and opens its wallet. Observe the dialogue customer has with the salesman; figure out the key words customer uses that will reveal what the customer wants. These details when rolled back into the system and acted upon by the team will make the difference to all the business and growth.

ACTIONABLE

**Get off your Arse,
be in the market place!**

Mind share before market share.
—Beth Comstock

13

Market Share

Mindless race to get ahead!

The race to get ahead of others to achieve higher Market share can be very destructive at times and this happens when the objective is single minded and has the blessings of CEO. This madness gets triggered when annual bonus of CEO gets decided on Market share or it's weightage on the to do list is higher than other parameters. All sorts of tricks, weapons in armoury are leashed out in the market place just to look at this market share percentage to go up by few percentages basis point.

Full back up support is provided to the front-line team just to get there. Caution is thrown to the winds and inventory is deliberately, forcefully and without application of mind is pushed to the reseller. All sorts of discounts, pricing gimmicks emerge on the horizon. Payment terms are relaxed. Front line officers are pressurized to the hilt and making their lives miserable. In between quick incentives get introduced for the team. In this melee the reseller who must sell to the consumer finds himself at the cross roads. Companies forget in this enthusiasm that secondary sales or tertiary sales are of utmost importance and unless goods move off the shelves, no purpose will be achieved. This finer point of Primary Vs Secondary and Tertiary sales is least understood or rather misunderstood.

First few months or few fortnights of the campaign to increase the market share are wonderful as transit pipelines are getting full and everyone feels happy and system is in a congratulatory mode and patting themselves on the back for outstanding achievement.

Here the inventory is shifting from Company ware house to reseller. Madness gets aggravated when gain on the inventory due to price rise accrue to the reseller. On a rising price curve, inventory shifts rapidly from manufacturer to reseller. Financial year over, results declared, market share up, outstanding up, relations with the reseller are at its worst as money to be realized is stuck in the pipeline. Primary sales for next few months have already been registered in earlier months.

No one in the system objects or has the guts to tell the Boss that what we are doing is improper. Understanding in the system is limited to the extent that you can make temporary gains with market share which will vanish sooner than later. Prepare a business plan which impacts your secondary or tertiary sales. Market share will improve on its own once secondary or tertiary sales are improved.

Skill sets of the team will leapfrog to the next level once team is asked to focus on secondary sales, reseller will love it and participate in the mission with full zeal. Most of the companies look down upon reseller as a step below partner whereas it should be other way round. In conclusion be aware of the pitfalls in increasing market share by increasing primary sales. Always keep bottom line in picture. Market share alone does not mean anything, if you have huge recoverable from the market.

NB: Primary sales are movement of product from company warehouse to reseller warehouse and secondary sales is to the ultimate user, customer from reseller.

Your professional skill sets will improve only if you put efforts to increase secondary or tertiary sale and not primary sales!

I read a book twice as fast as anybody else.
First, I read the beginning, and then I read
the ending, and then I start in the middle
and read toward whatever end I like best.
—Gracie Allen

Read Fast

You will be able to act faster!

As a professional irrespective of your trade in which you are practising, you often need to read documents. They can be of different types depending on kind of assignment you are engaged in on day to day basis. You read newspapers to begin with, multiple emails you receive during the day, dozens of SMSs, notifications from news, alerts from banks and many other text messages seek your attention. Your ability to read fast, your ability to retain, and recall what you have read will give you a cutting edge over many others.

This habit can be developed over a period. Just because you read and read fast, your ability to speak, hold crucial conversations and build your network will go up significantly. It is said that average rate of reading is say between 200-250 words per minute for a printed text and this reduces by around 10- 15 percent in case of reading on a computer. Let's get back to how you can read faster:

- ▶ All of us read with vocalization of words silently in our heart, which is time consuming and can it be minimized.

- ▶ There are many distractions in the process of reading, like phone calls, SMS etc, whether they can be eliminated by putting these things in silent mode.

- ▶ Can you do the block reading like reading few words together with a peripheral vision.

- ▶ Can you scan the entire document visually first and then important paras and make a mental note of important words in between. Visually scanning of the document first will give you a fair idea about the information you are going to receive after reading the document. It's like watching the trailer of a movie which gives the sense of the entire movie in few minutes, whether it's a romantic love story, sci-fi, comedy, adventure, guns and girls, tell-tale, or crime story or any other. You decide, based on your interest whether to see the movie or not.

▶ At times reading with the help of a pointer or moving your finger along can increase your speed. Some people use a blank paper as a tool to move along the lines.

▶ Besides reading faster your ability to recall what you have read makes the difference. Can you practise this and work regularly to improve this habit with a conscious mind?

On an average a book has say around 60,000 words and at the speed of 200 words per minute, you need 300 minutes for reading a book. Therefore, in five hours a book can be finished. If you allocate at least 45 minutes of focussed time on daily basis to read, you are through with the book in 6/7 days. To be a good reader you need to allocate a slot of time on daily basis and you should be mentally most agile at that time. This habit is like time spent in a physical gym on daily basis. Call it as your visit to mental gym and it is as essential as going to a gym for physical exercise. In today's world, it is necessary to be mentally fit besides being physically fit. Both kinds of fitness need equal and undivided attention.

Reading a book before going to sleep may not be the most productive way of developing reading habit.

I have seen and worked with few accomplished managers who are able to sign a long document and give their consent by quickly doing a mental scan of the few paragraphs like introduction and conclusion. Their ability to disagree and put a dissent note then and there was equally fast. As you grow in the hierarchy, you need to read more, give your consent either way and if you are a poor reader or who takes lot of time, obviously as a result of slow speed of reading, decision making and consequent speed of execution by your team will be really slow and sluggish and entire discredit will be on your door step. Be aware. There is a saying that there is no difference between persons who cannot read and who do not read.

ACTIONABLE **Leaders are readers. Are you one? If not, be one!**

Salary is a bribe that you get to forget your dreams. Choose a job you love, and you will never have to work a day in your life.
—Unknown

15

How Long your Job is Going to Last?

Ask this question regularly to yourself?

Going forward, four decades of active professional life (assuming you start after graduation and end up at 60) is a long period to survive with present rate and pace of change. With life expectancy going up, you can add another decade to your active professional life. Now whether you are at the beginning of your career, midpoint or at later stage, you have a challenge at your hand.

World is changing so rapidly that you never know when your professional life will take a turn. So long it is on the uptrend its good, but we all need to be fully aware of the circumstances, around us in our business and in official matters. Good change can be that your boss resigns, and you are asked to step in and take his position. Good change is your company is getting merged and you get a better and bigger role in the new set up. Good change is you get relocated to a place of your choice. Good change is you get few jumps in your position in the industry you are in.

On the downside, your skill sets may not be needed as product you are engaged in for selling or manufacturing is no more needed or the service you are engaged is automated. Impact is being seen regularly in all sectors, be it manufacturing, IT, automotive, financial, HR, sales, services sector, bank tellers, financial analysts, inventory managers, stockists, and construction workers. Few examples of certain jobs that have ceased to exist or are already in dustbin are office clerks, stenographers, mail sorters, ticketing and hotel booking.

If your industry deals with data or transactions of any kind, it will get disrupted by blockchain technology. With block chain technology on the horizon, fundamental principles on which banking, insurance, supply chain, health care, energy management, networking, internet of things, music, retail, and real estate's sector operates will alter so much that present incumbents doing repeatedly the same job year after year may find themselves at crossroads of their career sooner than later. Ask the person in the mirror the following questions:

- ▶ Are you doing the same job year after year?
- ▶ Are you willing to start all over again and drop your present baggage now and here?
- ▶ Have you ever been involved in a project which gave you an experience of different kind?
- ▶ Have you ever launched a new product or introduced a newer way of working?
- ▶ Are you comfortable with sudden changes in the routine which requires adjustments in personal and professional life?

How confident you are in retaining and growing with your present job. Take next steps in building your skill sets before it becomes rather late and you find yourself at cross roads.

According to World Economic Forum (WEF), skill sets needed in times to come or in the near future will be:

1. Complex problem solving.
2. Critical thinking.
3. Creativity.
4. People management.
5. Coordinating with others.
6. Emotional Intelligence.
7. Judgement & decision making.
8. Service orientation.

9. Negotiation.
10. Cognitive flexibility.

ACTIONABLE   **What is your agenda for learning this month, quarter or this year? Go and ask the man in the Mirror!**

Your network is your net worth.
— Portergale

16

It is Not what you Know but who you Know?

Connect, connect and connect

While in academics what you know will take you far ahead of others in all sorts of examination be written or oral, be it a class test or semester or final examination. All efforts in academic life are towards enhancing your capabilities in the subject you are pursuing. While stepping in corporate life you need to change gears and change them fast. Have seen many young guys continuing their academic habits for good number of years and then finding it extremely difficult to figure out as to what is needed here in this world of hard-core professionals competing rather vigorously. In corporate world you need to hit the radar as early as possible otherwise time just flies away. Hitting the radar means that you are known to persons who decide the fate of others. It can be your boss's boss, it can be the head of department, it can be the director on the board, and it can be the owner of the company in case of a privately held company. First and foremost, figure out with your own power of observation as to who matters the most on such issues. Let's call him Mr. X. All persons irrespective of their positions who have to decide critical issues in the company have a sounding board. This is the person (Let's call him Mr. Y) whose opinion is generally asked for and his words will make the difference and can be the deciding factor. This person can swing things in your favour or against you depending upon various factors which include his personal integrity. How is his position in the company on his personal growth? How much is his hold on business matters? Has he reached this position on merit or manipulation?

Now you need to seize the opportunity as and when it comes to hit the radar of Mr. X and Mr. Y. The opportunity can come in the lift, in lunch hour in canteen, in parking lot, travelling together in car, rail or plane, in a formal or an informal get together and of course most of the opportunities arise in business meetings. Now business meetings can be internal or with the customer and when Mr. X or Mr.Y is present and is leading the team for negotiating with the customer or discussing business plan internally. You will hit the radar early and repeatedly in case you are fully prepared on each point of the agenda of the meeting with all the pros and cons on your fingertips.

Your ability to speak or interject if invited and when you see an opportunity which is without invitation will make the difference. What you speak and if it is with full preparation and covers all the possible aspects, in a brief and in style and in a manner that moves the heads and you are heard with full attention and in pin drop silence, you have made your mark and hit the radar. You will know for yourself whether you have hit the radar or lost the opportunity. You need to speak extempore without any reference to any paper or shuffling your computer screen.

In this context Late Mr. Dhirubhai Ambani founder of Reliance Industries Ltd was never prepared to listen to an explanation or an answer which was given after referring to written notes or files in a meeting. His take was simple that you are not prepared well, or you do not know the subject well if you need to refer to a document for a matter which is your day to day business issue. The issue under discussion can be a simple question of what were sales last Month. Now you knowing the right man or his remembering you will make lots of difference in times to come whenever a selection is to me made for; be it a foreign trip, an advanced training program, just a fun tour, promotions and many other such benefits.

Consider and aim at hitting the radar very early in your career. Radar can undergo a change every year as promotions and transfers take place and newer persons move in. You will have to reposition yourself quickly before it gets late. You may have to work hard, spend more time in the office, just to get the right chance and opportunity. Ensure that you grasp the first available opportunity on the horizon and keep doing it whenever and wherever needed. You need to try all the time even if you have missed first few chances. All successful guys whose radar you should be are the guys who love meeting people, especially the newer people who bring in fresh perspective on the table. If you are not on the radar of right persons year after year, don't blame the environment for not giving you chance.

I recall an incident of my hitting the radar few years back while I was in front line position, I was asked to reach early to the office as real big boss had to come for a visit to see our preparedness for the upcoming commissioning of the plant. I happened to reach earlier than the scheduled time. My immediate boss who was to take the big boss around, arrived much later than the big boss, and he happened to reach earlier. In those days traffic congestion was not an excuse one could give, as on Delhi roads one could drive at the speed one wanted to. This was in 1981. My Royal Enfield mini bullet was my ever-dependent mate in those days. I had the privilege of taking the big boss around the plant as he was in a hurry and did not want to wait for my boss. Next fifteen minutes changed the course of my life and I was moved from there, a plant job, a very repetitive job, to a job and a function which I wanted and was not able to get it despite my many requests made through the routine channels.

Order of my transfer was issued in a matter of minutes. All colleagues of mine kept wondering as to what transpired in those few minutes of my being with big boss. It was just a plain conversation with the person who mattered the most and he readily accepted my request. Approaching the real big boss may have otherwise taken few years for me due to the layers above me.

Be in readiness always and every day, you never know when the opportunity may come, it will come unannounced and you should grasp it with both the hands like cricketers do while standing in slips position for a fast bowler.

Every day step out as if you are going for an interview and you may find that person at next crossing, which may change your life!

You are what you do,
not what you say you will do.
—Anonymous

Visiting Card?

Your gateway to net working

*Y*our visiting card is an instrument or a tool that works in many ways in personal and professional life. Not having a visiting card or having one and not carrying it for the important events or meetings is a mistake that can be costly for your professional and personal growth. You may miss an important opportunity or may miss an important piece of information or some further business proposals in the near future. Your visiting card with your name, designation, company's name and logo, your contact detail by way of phone and e-mail, web address is good enough for all purposes. Simple visiting cards are appreciated more. The life of card is the time which elapses between handing over the card and when first contact is made thru mobile or email etc. Thereafter it vanishes into some corner of your work station. A visiting card serves many purposes like

- ▶ Your introduction in a jiffy.
- ▶ Your company's brand awareness.
- ▶ Your credibility as a professional manager.
- ▶ Your first impressions.
- ▶ It is a low- cost marketing tool.
- ▶ Ice breaker for discussions.

While it's important that you carry your card, but you must hand over the card to a person with full attention of your body with respectful gestures. Similarly receive the card with full gratitude and express that in words as well. Never ever write anything on some one's card in his presence, which generally people do to put some information. It's simply a bad manner to put it with candour.

There are occasions when you need to hand over the card first to make a contact in which you have interest. But do reciprocate when you are handed over the card first. Be generous in sharing your card with as many persons to increase your network. Not everyone will get connected with you in short term, but in long run, a card exchanged will not be a wasted opportunity as cards do get handed over to the successors at times in the company and your connect will remain.

Change of job, change of location or change of department in the same company will need newer cards. Never write anything on your card and give it to any one since there was a change in your designation or address or contact coordinates. It's unprofessional and hits your credibility. It does not take long to print cards these days.

With use of faster means of communication like mobile phone and WhatsApp therein, LinkedIn, Messenger, Twitter, use of visiting card is considerably reduced but they have not become extinct and are still relevant in the professional circles.

ACTIONABLE

Your visiting card is your ID in corporate circus!

The key to success is to keep growing in all areas of life mental, emotional, spiritual, as well as physical.

—Julius Erving

18

Are you Growing?

Growing is a way of life

*I*ts a serious question one must ask every day to one self. Are you growing day by day physically or you have also grown on many other aspects which impact your life? Are you growing only by number of days or your mental capital is also growing faster. Growth is the way of life and unless you are growing mentally, financially, socially, intellectually with physical age, there can be serious issue as time flies very fast and very soon you can be the last man in the queue that will get longer and longer with persons joining ahead of you in the queue.

In corporate world there is no rule that you can join the queue only at the end, you can be placed on top of the queue depending upon your capabilities. It is your own determination which will pave the way for growth. Let us answer the following questions w.r.t your status today in comparison to your status a year back:

- ▶ Is your network the same as it was, how many more have you added or deleted?
- ▶ Are you in a position to work on lap top much more easily all by yourself or you need help?
- ▶ Has your relation with your boss improved from where it was earlier? Have you learnt to manage your boss?
- ▶ Have you improved on your public speaking skills, are you in a position to speak extempore?
- ▶ Are you delegating more than you were earlier?

- ▶ Is your indispensability far less than it was earlier?
- ▶ Are you able to read faster, are you able to listen faster?
- ▶ Are you able to manage your time better than earlier?
- ▶ Have your etiquettes on social front shown a drastic improvement?
- ▶ Has your general awareness on PESTLE (PESTLE is a mnemonic which in its expanded form denotes P for Political, E for Economic, S for Social, T for Technological, L for Legal and E for Environmental. At times E also gets referred as Ethical) improved?
- ▶ Are you spending more time in the market place and less before the screen?
- ▶ Are you in a better control of your finances?
- ▶ Have you chosen to mentor someone or you have become a mentee yourself?
- ▶ Do you have a fair idea as to whether you are employed or employable?
- ▶ Are you aware as to how long your job is going to last?
- ▶ What is your market value today and what it was last year?

Questions can be endless and depending upon your curiosity and anxiety and concern for growth you will not only frame questions to yourself but also find answers to them in the most professional manner.

Growing in experience year after year on the same job, growing in designation year after year without your intrinsic mental growth, without your network growth, without your improvement in skills like speaking, articulating, reading, listening, mentoring, and helping others is a false growth.

You are cheating yourself if you are doing the same work which you were doing earlier after you got promoted. You must make a commitment to yourself that all those things which you were doing earlier; you will not do in your elevated position and will down delegate the same. Not many people do so for fear of job insecurity and find themselves competing with juniors and then starts the downward spiral. Persons start on path downhill.

Develop a plan of the parameters you wish to improve upon in a time bound manner.

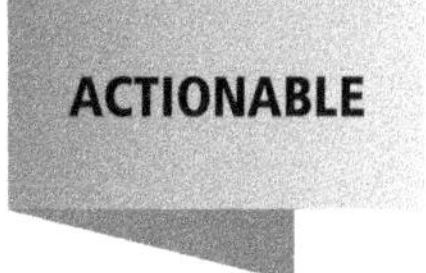

Write down your own appraisal every month, quarter and year as CEO of your company self Inc!

More you learn, more you earn!
—Warren Buffet

19

Your Mental Capital

More valuable than financial capital

*I*n Wikipedia definition it means the degree of mastery of life skills at the time an Individual faces the choice of life. It is an immaterial economic capital. How do you make the most of yourself in the 21st century with your mental capital? How well you can contribute to your professional life, society and your personal life. Word Capital here sparks association with your financial capital, like your financial capital which needs to grow to beat inflation, for which we make all efforts most of the time and perhaps all the time.

Make an earnest attempt to grow your mental capital with time. Unlike financial capital, your mental capital grows rapidly when you share your knowledge, experience and skill sets with others. I have always experienced that while taking sessions on any subject with large audience, questions which get asked always lead to some addition to the mental capital. A new perspective emerges on the horizon. Not sharing your mental capital can lead to its deterioration and will only contract over a period.

With changing lifestyles, changes in technology and better life expectancy addition to the mental capital needs to be also fast. If you are still visiting banks for daily needs, still visiting utilities to pay bills, still looking for an insurance agent, still visiting broker for stock market transactions, still on a feature phone, still hand write a note and then seek assistance for it to be typed, still go around physically to buy ticket for a sports event, movie or play or trip to domestic or overseas location, still need to open your laptop to see your mails, still need to carry lots of cash, still using a physical diary to note the important dates, still asking people the route to your destination within your city, then do take a stock of the situation with the man in the mirror.

And for the people who are not doing all above, what are the plans to understand impact of Artificial intelligence on your job? Is block chain technology worth spending time on? Is virtual and augmented reality making difference to your life? Is social media relevant for your professional and personal brand?

Let's be conscious of the fact that your mental capital needs to grow and only your mental capital can grow your financial capital and not the other way round. All what is needed is commitment and passion to grow your mental capital to remain relevant in social and professional life in future and for all times to come.

ACTIONABLE   **Identify first and eliminate all your weaknesses one at a time in a time bound manner!**

The key to success is to keep growing in all areas of life mental, emotional, spiritual, as well as physical

—Julius Erving

Interval

Time to change gears

Like movies, plays and sports each professional career also has interval time. Before the interval, generally different characters get introduced and established. Professionals get differentiated, labelled and are earmarked for possible roles in the future.

Assuming in a company, there are 10 steps to reach the board position, your journey after 5th step will become harder and harder. The skill sets acquired & demonstrated in first five steps may no longer be useful, you may have to quickly unlearn and relearn few things from your seniors. Journey becomes harder as the organizational pyramid becomes narrower as you travel up. After the interval at each step persons in the race start falling on the way side one after the other.

Reasons for falling can be very personal at times. There are compulsions for certain people for family reasons like spouse employment, parents' care, child education etc. to not to leave a place and, therefore, further progress is impacted. Fatigue, lack of ambition, inadequate fitness, being happy in a comfort zone, delivering or just meeting the minimum expected standards year after year, not taking enough risks, always blaming others are some other reasons for falling by the way side. Professional reasons to fall on the way side after the interval can be many more like,

▶ Questionable integrity.

- ► Lack of proper etiquette.
- ► Inability to assert.
- ► No backbone for decision making.
- ► I and not we attitude.
- ► Inability to get along with counterparts and seniors.
- ► Lack of Trust.
- ► Lack of Customer care.
- ► Unable to dive deeper and deeper.
- ► Making things complex instead of simplifying.
- ► Unable to stick to business plan formulated year after year and then go off course.
- ► Results and goals missed.

In case you are observant enough during your journey up to the interval, you will certainly develop those etiquettes, behaviour, emotional intelligence, traits of the senior persons who are on the fast track. You would be in that select group of people who are certainly going to hit the top position. Soon after the interval you will be on the radar of the persons who are actively involved in succession plan of the organization.

All professional organizations which last for years have a very structured way of doing it without the incumbents even noticing it till very late stage. That is for natural progress of the person with all his ambitions and learning to get acquired on the way.

It was my privilege to see the annual report of a senior manager where the eminent director on the board had stated that he be nurtured for the board position. This remark was made at least 15 years ahead of the person reaching the board position. All went well, and the officer is on a board position now.

Above is true for the companies where lateral hiring is minimal and home-grown talent is considered to be the best. In case you have just started your career or are on first or second step, be on the lookout for the seniors getting ready for post interval life. Find ways to spend time with them. Always be in the company of the professionals from whom the learning to you comes naturally, whose visibility in the organisation for right reasons is very high and are seen in the company of the persons deciding the future of organisation and people.

Certain companies fill up the senior positions wherein the talent is brought from outside. Here again only those persons get parachuted who have been able to hit the radar after the interval in their earlier careers.

ACTIONABLE   **Pause, reflect, and plan your next steps for final journey to the top!**

Grudging compliance will not
take you anywhere
—Anonymous

21

Are you Mr 100%?

60/70/80/90 % will not do!

You need to take full ownership of the job you have been assigned to complete or the job you undertake yourself on your own volition. Everyone has different positions at different stages of career. You can be a part of the team or you can be the leader of the team depending on the situation. Giving one hundred percent is the attitude one needs to develop from early days in the career. There cannot be grudging compliance, it must be compliance with a smile, compliance with full heart and soul into it.

Example of one hundred percent from sports is that in cricket every batsman tends to finish the game with last winning run. Each batsman tries one after another, few succeed, and few fail. But the failed person in one inning succeeds in another inning. Attitude of one hundred percent remains imbibed deep down in the mind and body of each member of the team whether he is bowling, batting or fielding. In the corporate world, I have seen many professionals start discovering excuses ahead of time. They are more concerned on the likely explanation to be given if objective is not achieved. So, the race starts with a person as a loser and not as a likely contender who will win. He starts to discover what's wrong with environment who did not respond in time, lack of adequate tools to tackle the objective, inadequate travel and meeting arrangements, poor customer response, finds faults with government policies and regulators attitude to the market. These are some of very standardized excuses in corporate word. These are all Mr. 30/40/50 percent who lose out immediately after the interval.

Mr. One hundred percent will start with a list of likely show stoppers or road blocks which will be faced during the journey. List will be the same as of Mr. 30/40/50 percent but the way Mr. One hundred percent looks at it is totally different. He will be thoroughly immersed and keep his team engaged and will be on top of all issues. In corporate world either you have done it, or you have not done it. Also ran, tried, but failed, will get in the category of Mr. 30/40/50 percent. Appraisals and increments will be in accordance. You will have ample time further to discover false issues like why are you Mr. 30/40/50 percent. Sit back, relax, reflect, and refocus on the way you do things and get out of 30/40/50 percent bracket!

ACTIONABLE **Locate all show stoppers and find ways to dislodge them forever!**

Feeling gratitude and not expressing it is like wrapping a present and not giving it
—William Arthur Ward

22

Attitude of Gratitude (AOG)

Be grateful for small mercies!

This attribute will take you places. Express, record, speak and, acknowledge gratitude for the person who deserves and has made the difference in achieving the set target and goal. This is irrespective of the stage or position you are in. People remember this for life time and will perform much better without any prompt, persuasion or follow up. Express this publicly, don't hold yourself back, and be prepared to roll out good words appropriate for the person and the occasion.

I have seen performances skyrocketing to a different level when appreciation is conveyed with full conviction and body language is in sync with the words. It has long lasting impact. Once this habit is inculcated, words of positivity and gratitude will come out so naturally that you will not even feel it. Have seen very accomplished persons expressing it so effortlessly to even a door or lift man, driver, watchman, house help, street vendor, shopkeeper, shop or mall attendant, waiter, chef, bar man, office boy, team members and of course boss. It pays rich dividends in personal and professional life. It costs nothing. Even a good genuine smile in a manner that says it all is a gratitude expressed without opening your mouth. Just a nudge on the shoulder or gentle pat on the back is equally good.

On the contrary observe a person without attitude of gratitude in your office (you will find them in plenty). He along with his team will be struggling to meet the goals, loosing direction and with slower speed of work and grudging compliance. The services he receives from support staff will be delayed and thereby raising his blood pressure. Many of the professionals who reach a stage ahead of their peer group do develop this habit (of not expressing gratitude) and very soon the velocity of career is impacted. These professionals are arrogant and are very low on emotional intelligence.

With attitude of gratitude you will sleep better, relations will become robust, physical health will improve and your habit will be infectious and others will follow. You will be remembered for times to come in the profession and industry.

In very early stages of my career, just a year or two after the academics, I recall a very senior accomplished professional holding door for me and putting his hand on my shoulder in most respectful way to enter the meeting room wherein he was the boss and I was just a small fry who was not expected to open his mouth and just hold the pen and paper for recording the discussions. This act of his though a small gesture made me feel so good about him and whenever we met again, I was always on the lookout for reciprocating his gesture. AoG goes a long way.

ACTIONABLE — **Let your body be in perfect sync with words you utter to express gratitude. Needs practise!**

"*I don't trust anyone who doesn't laugh.*"
—Maya Angelou

23

Humour Makes the Difference

Timing is equally important!

Post lunch hour most of the offices are low on efficiency and generally the response level is sluggish. If you have to address a class or chair a meeting or attend a meeting post lunch, there will be big challenge to keep the persons engaged all the time. Start with a good humour appropriate for the occasion, well timed, short and sweet and you will win half the battle. It's true for everyone including you. After good lunch body and mind are in sync to relax but professional compulsions are otherwise to attend to many important issues and deliver on the commitments.

In one of the lectures I attended long back, the speaker was smart enough to say in the beginning that should you fall asleep, please don't snore as a consideration for others.

He narrated an incident where one person during his long lecture, literally fell asleep and started snoring. He admits having asked person sitting next to him to shake him and wake him up. Promptly he got a reply that you have put him to sleep now you have to wake him up. That sent the class rolling into laughter and his task was made easier for next few hours. Every 15 or 20 minutes he will make Interjection with lots of humour to keep everybody engaged and hooked on to him.

Always rehearse before any presentation to invoke humour at the appropriate moment, be at beginning or middle or at the end. It requires hard work, preparation and understanding of the current events to juxtapose the humour into the business. Some of the most difficult moments and crucial conversations have been made easier with light-hearted banter and humour which is timely, and not gender biased or related to any cast, creed or religion. You need to be very sensitive of these parameters while invoking humour.

While preparation for the business is needed all the time, look for the appropriate humour alongside. Humour need to be timed well, according to the circumstances and events. Joking about World Cup while football is the flavour or Cricket or whichever sports or event is going on, will quickly connect you with your audience.

Well placed humour which does not hurt the sentiment of any person from any country will increase your likability index in your network to a much higher level resulting in ease of dialogue, negotiation and making your point across.

ACTIONABLE   **Develop sense of humour appropriate for each occasion!**

People buy into the leader before they
buy into the vision
—John C Maxwell

24

Buy in

Debate before deciding

*A*ll decisions taken in corporate world do not get implemented in letter and spirit in an organization. Assuming that at team level, certain decision is taken in isolation, without any discussion with other team members, by you as a team leader and is conveyed to the team for immediate implementation. There would obviously be lots of questions valid or otherwise by the members in their mind. Depending upon your image or your personal credibility it will be weighed from the perspective of

- ▶ Is it good for the company?
- ▶ Is it good for the team?

Or

Is it good only for you as a team leader?

It is always appropriate that each decision taken and conveyed has a full buy in from all the members in team from their perspective. It's a good idea to discuss face to face on when, why, where, and how of all the changes. Power of persuasion and effort is needed to convince the team as to how the company, team and individuals will be benefited by the decision taken.

Generally, those decisions which are not debated upon before implementation do not get executed with full vigour and there is a grudging compliance by the team. Members are not able to figure out as to why they are doing what they are doing. Let us appreciate that you have taken onboard very smart and efficient people and they are here to add value to the company, team and themselves in that order and not the other way round. They are fully aware that success of the company on certain deliverables will bring laurels to the team and the individuals CV as well. Lack of information, not sharing of information can lead to less than needed inputs, actions, and less involvement by the members of the team and it will yield sub optimal results.

Always ensure that there is a buy in at all levels for all new initiatives, changes proposed in work environment, policy changes affecting the life style of individuals and many other issues of significant importance.

ACTIONABLE   **Power to persuade is needed at all levels. Develop it as early as you can!**

Do not speak ill of your predecessors or successors. You did not walk in their shoes.
— Donald Rumsfeld

25

Never Blame your Predecessor

You will only hurt yourself

*I*n a long service period of 35 plus years, assuming you start at the age of 25 you change positions, places, departments and locations and you are a successor at the new place or predecessor at the old place where from you have moved out. Each new place will throw up new challenges of work culture especially in large companies. Work culture which includes attitude towards timing, seniors, colleagues, peers, goal setting, and execution varies considerably from region to region or division to division.

Variations will be apparent in the working at headquarters, regions and say zonal office. This is within the same company and irrespective of what is written in the rule book.

When you change position as a team leader, your new team will need few adjustments depending upon your personal preferences on small things like you may prefer all meetings before lunch, no meetings on Monday and Friday, only working lunch and not any elaborate ones if at all need to be hosted, no ppts only a word document, and time allocated for the meeting, on the contrary your predecessor may have had different preferences altogether. Such changes do create murmur as all team members need to readjust to the new ways of working.

There is nothing wrong in small changes of above parameters. Some not so matured leaders engage themselves in open and wide criticism of the past habits of their predecessor on the small issues as mentioned above. In addition, whatever wrong is discovered, there is a tendency to blame the predecessor all the time and most of the time.

Blaming the predecessor is a habit which is self-destructive and exposes more your weakness in accepting the ground reality. You never know under what circumstances, market conditions, delivery schedules, inventory conditions, competitive landscape your predecessor faced in his tenure. It's your battle now, it's your team now, don't ever look at the rear-view mirror, what's gone is gone, just keep moving forward.

Blaming the predecessor amounts to criticizing the entire team of their past deeds and some of the members can suddenly feel dejected by your uttering. They may also feel that your criticisms are directed towards them. Now same thing can happen to you at the place you have left. Similar dialogues or uttering by your successor may be taking place there as well.

I have seen some very mature and accomplished leaders from close quarters at a very senior level who will never give their reactions or feelings or judgements on the past ways of working for getting results or on strategies adopted by predecessor for day to day operational deliverables. It is done and over. Look ahead and keep going without looking into past. It will only hurt you, your personal reputation, your relations, team spirit and the overall efficiency.

It is always good to pick up some good points from your predecessors' innings and build on that. There will be quite a few strong points where team may have excelled. At times despite the best of the efforts by the team, market conditions and headwinds, results did not emerge and the whole tenure went as a non-performance.

Such habit of blaming the predecessor can also be interpreted in many ways. Your competence for the job is limited and you are not able to see beyond tomorrow. You are an expert who lives in the past. Blame the predecessor at your own peril.

ACTIONABLE   **Whatever be the circumstances always look ahead!**

Time = life; therefore, waste your time and you waste your life, or master your time and master your life.
—Alan Lakein

26

Time Management

Improve your personal life

You must assess and tell yourself the value of your time based on your position in the company and your job. Is it 1000 bucks per hour or 5000 bucks per hour? This is irrespective of the fact whether you are self-employed or working for some one. An assessment here can mean a lot for your esteem and consequential actions of yours during the day and days thereafter for all times to come.

Time management is a very significant and important part of personal and professional life. All accomplished persons who have done exceedingly well in their professional life attach very high importance to this attribute.

Let us say that you spend considerable time in the office and always come home late because of pressures of work. Just reflect, whether you're coming back late to your house is for reasons that can be attributed to you or someone else is not supporting you for the work to be completed in time.

In case you're coming home late day after day is for reasons entirely of your own, there is a need for you to relook as to how you are managing your time. Let us look at few issues given below:

- ▶ Are you engaging yourself in procrastination?
- ▶ Are you taking longer time than required for a meeting chaired by you?
- ▶ Do you get called for the meetings without any prior notice?

- ▶ Do you attend meetings where you are not needed at all?
- ▶ Are your telephone conversations unduly long?
- ▶ Do you get calls at unexpected hours?
- ▶ Do you digress from the main issues?
- ▶ Are you suffering from verbal diarrhoea or mental constipation?
- ▶ Do you get visitors without any notice?
- ▶ Are you not able to down delegate for fear of losing importance? Do you engage in work of juniors?
- ▶ Are you competing with your juniors?
- ▶ Are you in a position to say no wherever and whenever needed?

These are all controllable items and you should have full command on time as far as these issues or concerned. An unexpected call from the boss can spoil your day and upset the entire schedule for the remaining part of the day. It is always good to expect such moves and budget your time for them though, it is always not possible.

A very senior boss of mine was in the habit of coming late to the office and he would also go back late from work. Brilliant person he was, whose professional competence was way ahead of others. Work load on him was high and he was managing his time so well. Since he was in a very senior position, all juniors will wait for him to leave office. Whether Junior is required or not, irrespective of the need most of them will go home only after the he has gone. There was no requirement or expectation from the boss for people to wait. Persons had inflicted injury on themselves waiting for hours without any professional reasons. It was just to impress the boss. Once when asked privately that lots of people wait for you to go home before they go home, he laughed and said what I can do if they do not want to go home. If I need them I would certainly call or tell somebody that particular person should wait. At times some people hang around in the office and spoil their good family time for unknown reasons. Check it out. Are you one of them? There are very many and better ways to hit the radar and impress the boss rather than waiting for him to go home, before you can leave.

Talking about this person, his sense of time management was extremely high and some of the attributes which helped are as follows:

- ▶ Piss of people if they're not sticking to the subject or the time allotted.
- ▶ Don't let issues be digressed in professional meetings; this is the biggest menace in official life.
- ▶ Be brief in conversation.
- ▶ Listen fast.
- ▶ Return all the calls received at a time when you want to do and not when caller wants to speak.
- ▶ Prepare ahead of time by anticipating crisis.
- ▶ All schedules of work well planned every week in advance: Minimize interruptions from the boss by giving solutions ahead of time, and keep him in loop all the time on important issues.
- ▶ Always give a timeline for the job to be completed.

Make every minute count at work. Do not let your personal time be consumed by others inefficiency!

It's not enough to be busy, so are the ants. The question is, what are we busy about?
—Henry David Thoreau

27

I don't have Time

Busy man finds time!

While in professional life when to seek assistance or a clarification or some data you approach a colleague or peer or a senior, within the team or outside in a different function and you may get the following response

- ▶ Have no time.
- ▶ Let us discuss it next week.
- ▶ It is not my job.
- ▶ It is not relevant.
- ▶ Talk to my boss first.
- ▶ Come through proper channel.
- ▶ Send a mail with full background.

In most of the cases all the time and most of the time in all cases be assured that you are knocking at the wrong door. Person you have approached has no clue or answer to your needs and is just posturing. He doesn't know. These are self-centred, mentally constipated and insecure professional managers. They believe that sharing knowledge, information and data will reduce their importance in the hierarchy and reduce their chances of growth. Your repeated attempts with the person will be a waste of time, and he will talk to you on all other subjects than what you want to know. Review your relations with him, if he is high in your network list, bring him down few notches and eliminate him over a period.

My strong conviction is that a person who knows the subject feels elated when someone is seeking guidance from him. His mental makeup is one of giving, one of sharing. He believes that knowledge that he is sharing will be back with him sooner and with lots of value addition. It does happen that way. Many of the persons senior to me whom I worked with and who were ready to guide, share the information moved higher much faster than others who had no time for others.

Have also experienced that whenever you are asked to wait, intent of the person is to spend value time with you and you will come out fully satisfied from the meeting which gets held after a wait. Consider your own position as to how you deal with such situations when someone approaches you? Are you willing to share information, data and knowledge in a jiffy or you posture? Always have time for others and be ready to help. You will be benefitted. Try this out.

ACTIONABLE

Eliminate guys with attitude who say I have no time from your network!

By prevailing over all obstacles and
distractions, one may unfailingly arrive at his
chosen goal or destination.
—Christopher Columbus

28

Put off Notifications

Smart phone menace!

With the advent of smart phones, the way we work, the way we communicate has changed drastically. Each handheld phone serves multiple uses like:

- ▶ Notes.
- ▶ Emails.
- ▶ WhatsApp.
- ▶ Calculator.
- ▶ Weather.
- ▶ News.
- ▶ Twitter/ FB/Pinterest/Instagram.
- ▶ YouTube.
- ▶ Stock markets, Bookings, Shopping.
- ▶ Banks, Utilities for bill payments.
- ▶ Streaming of movies are some of the many facilities.

Items above have a capability of generating a notification which keeps popping up throughout the day on your hand-held device. These are time destroyers, attention diverters and can keep you distracted all the time. Your ability to concentrate on a given task will diminish to such an extent that you would end up spending much more time than what is required on a task you are engaged in. Quality of work will suffer, and you may not be able to deliver within the time frame required or promised.

Unless you are in a job which requires you to get information ahead of others, like in a stock market, it is advisable to keep the notifications off during the time you are at work or in discussions with a person or in a meeting with a number of people. Your ability to listen with attention will be impaired as too often you will be glancing at the phone. It can be very irritating for the person who is with you and your likability index can go down by few notches down and can impact your overall performance. Consider using phone with notifications disabled to have uninterrupted attention towards the work.

While multitasking may be a good habit but when you need a very focused time to dwell on issues of importance for you personally & professionally, keep notifications off or keep the phone itself locked up for the time you can afford it.

ACTIONABLE   **Are you in control or your phone is controlling you? Check often!**

"Opportunities don't happen.
You create them."
—Chris Grosser

29

Business Development

Key to learning

*E*ach company has its own way of deciding as to what is business development in their business context. The role in business development can be very challenging but very educative in professional life. It can give you an experience of different kind altogether, distinct from routine and repetitive jobs of operational nature. Business development job could encompass:

- ▶ Increasing revenue.
- ▶ Reducing cost.
- ▶ Develop a new customer segment.
- ▶ New product launch.
- ▶ Setting up a new Project.
- ▶ Setting a new department within a company for new business line.

Now to accomplish the above tasks, you are expected to be aware of many factors which impact the business. Some of the important factors are outlined below:

- ▶ Product specifications.
- ▶ Supply demand balance.
- ▶ Potential forecast.
- ▶ Cost and Pricing.
- ▶ Competition.
- ▶ Manufacturers, Suppliers.
- ▶ Regulatory aspects.

- ▸ Customer preferences.
- ▸ Overall Market intelligence.
- ▸ Land requirement.
- ▸ Capital and operating cost.
- ▸ Time lines.

Job in business development requires lots of patience as there can be days altogether where no action can be taken. It's different from an operation job wherein actions are required to be taken every hour of the day and there is never a dull moment. Businesses are developed on assumptions made on many factors some of which are listed above. The assumptions can go wrong as everyone's ability to foresee into future is limited. Assumptions going wrong are part of professional hazard and one should be ready for a course correction whenever and wherever needed. Examples below are illustrations of assumptions going wrong in professional work.

A few million-dollar project, which had gestation period of 36 months, assumption was made that entire produce will be exported as domestic demand was fully saturated by existing suppliers. On inception of the project, all assumptions and projections made by subject experts, consultants, bankers, marketers and many others were thrown out of the window. Not even a single molecule of the product was needed for export. At that point of time potential for sales available in domestic market was much more favourable for the project, (though exactly opposite to what was assumed), and therefore no questions were raised

In yet another case of a large project an assumption was made that currency exchange rate will fluctuate in one direction making it more difficult for the project to survive. In reality currency exchange rate moved in a direction more favourable for the project.

At a given time when project is to be approved bias and mind set in business development team is different. Business management team may have to develop different work plans to go to market on different realties altogether from the ones assumed by business development team.

Irrespective of the role you are in, whether in business development or business management, your ability to quickly realign with ground realties will only make you a front runner or you will be doing a post-mortem or engage in a blame game with the previous team. Never, ever blame your predecessors.

Be ready for course correction. Professional journey is full of detours!

Once you see the boundaries of your environment, they are no longer the boundaries of your environment.
—Marshall McLuhan

30

Boundary Management

Face to face not Facebook

*I*n corporate world you cannot, and you should not work in isolation. You need constant inputs from all departments for a task to be completed. Assuming you are in sales job which requires an immaculate on the stage performance before the customer. For you to deliver a good performance all back-stage performers say pricing, finance, quality control, manufacturing, warehouse, logistics, and personnel should be in total sync with you. In the event of any one not joining the party, your performance can go wrong.

On the flip side in case you're not rolling back the information which customers generally provide in plenty to the right person in the back stage be it on pricing, quality, packaging or others; it can lead the team performance going down rapidly. Sharing information will lift the overall morale of the team. Boundary management is necessary in this context of business. Not all matters can be put in black and white and, therefore, it becomes necessary to meet face to face with persons on the back stage. I have seen few accomplished persons commencing their day first by meeting all the concerned persons and thereafter responding to their mails or messages. Meeting people face to face will ease your day to day issues and will surely enhance your performance. Now these regular meetings will facilitate interpersonal relations reach a stage where all communication barriers are broken, no formalities are observed during interaction and resolution of issues is achieved in no time. Mind you, in such meetings you need to leave the person in a much better position than you found him.

In case you can leave the person happier than you found him, be sure that your boundary management approach is working and will deliver results faster than expected. This is true for both on official and personal matters. Irrespective of the position you are in, leave your work station, and leave your cabin at least once in a day to go around, meet and greet people. Discuss the topic of another person's interest. Listen more and talk less. Hear what the body is saying as everyone is not good at articulating what he/she wants to convey. Boundary management will enhance your likability index which is a prerequisite for any task to be carried out by the team.

Boundary management is required to be done with all stake holders be it internal or external. This is an essential task to be completed for any deliverables to be made in the time frame and at agreed cost parameters. Boundary management will only increase the speed of the business; it will reduce the cost of the business. It will develop your network for all your future projects.

ACTIONABLE

Mails alone cannot resolve issues. Meeting in person often helps in taking next steps!

Show your instructions in actions as much as you can.
—Catherine Macaulay

31

Put your Pen where your Mouth is

Never give instructions which you will not like to execute yourself

As a team leader or as a member of a team, lots of interactions take place on daily basis by word of mouth, in writing on mails, by body signals and other latest means of communication of your hand-held phones like SMS, WhatsApp, Messenger and others. Over a period, e-mails, SMSs have been reduced and are replaced by WhatsApp for ease and speed of communicating. Oral or spoken messages are getting reduced day by day. For sake of good order all communications to the field or large teams should be in writing. It helps.

- ▶ Everyone gets the same communication and implementation is easier.
- ▶ Any follow up clarifications and amendments are known to everyone.
- ▶ No one has the risk of missing vital points.
- ▶ Trust within the team stays at high standard.

Over smart executives especially in big companies at times to ensure that information does not get leaked to competition or no claims are raised against the company tend to convey things orally. Simultaneously they take a position that verbal instructions given by them cannot be confirmed on mail even by the listener or recipient of instructions. Seeds of mistrust are sown there itself. Everyone has a question on mind what if anything goes wrong, Buck will stop where?

Examples can be of financial incentives to front line executives or to resellers on achieving a sales performance, subject to meeting few conditions. At times it is done in anticipation of approval from higher management to save time or commence actions on time. More often than once all verbal information on important issues gets garbled and interpreted in a manner which suits the individual and claims are made accordingly. On completion of the incentive period say which is a quarter or six months, claims are made, get disputed for one reason or the other as everyone has its own interpretation on finer points. And then and their mistrust starts between colleagues, offices and stake holders, and thereafter people start demanding that in future everything be put it in black and white. Matter gets further complicated when higher office is not able to secure the approval of relevant authority and over smart executive comes out of the situation as he is in higher office and thus trust of team is lost forever. Whatever you could do in seconds will now take hours.

Whatever was possible by word of mouth earlier is not possible now. Whatever was not needed to put in writing earlier is required to be put in writing now.

Never ever give instructions which cannot be put in writing or which cannot be confirmed back or documented to you by the recipient. It's improper. It is breach of trust. It is fatal. You will lose all your credibility in no time and journey after the interval will become much harder and will be full of road blocks.

Always give recordable instructions!

'My idea of good company…is the company of clever, well-informed people, who have a great deal of conversation; that is what I call good company' 'You are mistaken,' said he gently, 'that is not good' company, that is the best."
— Jane Austen, Persuasion

32

Review your Network

What is your networkability index?

Developing a solid network of friends, professionals in your trade or outside, in the industry you are in, in your company, in your neighbourhood can give you an added advantage and cutting edge over the peers. Your life can be much fruitful and easier in case you have friends all around. Advantages of a good network will mean

- ► Many career opportunities can fall in your lap.
- ► Ease in approaching the right person.
- ► Information sharing.
- ► Credibility and Confidence.
- ► Learning from others' experience.
- ► Help in case of unfortunate events.
- ► Personal and Company's promotion.

While you develop the network for overall growth for personal and professional needs, one needs to review quite regularly whether the persons in your network are toxic, are not yes man, can give divergent views, are able to dissent, are not who want to keep you happy all the time, are not envious of your progress in life. They are not taking undue advantage of your position in professional and personal life. These are some of the questions you need to ask yourself.

Occasionally it's a good idea to check and find the usefulness of the network you have. Be mindful that it works both ways; someone else would be checking usefulness of yours and your ability to respond to others. Your personal attitude to your network makes a difference on the quality of the network you may have. I have seen good relations of number of years getting snapped over small and trivial issues like delayed response, not honouring the invitations for functions of personal importance.

It takes lots of effort to sustain a network of large number of people across your professional circles. I have seen many successful professionals nurturing the network at huge costs even incurred from their personal money, spending considerable time in travelling to honour the received invites even at the cost of personal discomfort.

One of my senior's advice was that if you entertain your customer or a friend or an acquaintance at home with a cup of tea, he will feel much more obliged than a five-star dinner. People remember such acts of personal discomfort and hospitality offered for life time and are more obliged to reciprocate. Life is all about growth and you cannot grow in life without a network of friends, associates, peers, colleagues, seniors and many other acquaintances.

You need to find ways to grow your network and for doing so it's important that all relevant meetings, events, seminars and other such functions are attended. Never ever feel shy of knowing a person who is in the vicinity, you never know your next career move may be just with that person. Drop few persons from your network every year, test your network every now and then, it will be useful to undertake this exercise.

ACTIONABLE

Do check occasionally attitude of the person in your network. Review your list!

There is only one boss. The customer.
And he can fire everybody in the company
from the chairman to downwards, simply by
spending his money somewhere else.
— Sam Walton

Boss's Instructions

Never use your boss's name to get jobs done

Quite often the teams are communicated certain instructions which can be operative or strategic with a specific name attached to it as to who has said this. Generally, this name is of a very senior person in the hierarchy who may or may not have said or given such intrusions. This is generally done by the person whose personal reputation on deliverables are at stake, but his visibility with senior most person is on daily basis. This is done with a motive that attaching the name will break down all resistance or concerns any one may have and the task will get accomplished at a faster pace.

He knows that none other than him can approach the person whose name has been taken by him to convey instructions. Teams in good faith follow and execute the instructions earlier than needed as the credibility of the person whose name is thrown around is high. Over a period when this becomes a routine, then teams start discounting what is instructed with name associated of the senior person. This happens both in private and public sector. In private sector senior most, person is obviously the owner of the company and one is not sure whether he would have said this or not.

There can be two ways of looking at it. Whether the senior person really wants his name associated with it or it is a game plan of the person next to him. Either way it is improper. In case the company or the senior leadership have lost the art and patience of getting buy in at the level down below and if they feel all instructions with the name attached are good to go, things will go hay wire. It will work if you have recruited below average people in the organization who have no enthusiasm to discover the best, who always wait for the instructions to be implemented, right or wrong.

In case you have confidence in your teams, in case you have best of the talent in the hierarchy, show them respect by not throwing the name. Give them challenge and they will perform better than what is expected with instructions conveyed with the name attached.

Generally, the toxic boss likes his name attached to the instructions so that people in his coterie get the message loud and clear. Normally such instructions will be not for the benefit of the company but individual's benefit either of the person who is communicating or of the person whose name is thrown around.

Challenge, argue, persuade, and convince the team to perform. Do not attach names to the task to be accomplished!

*You are serving a customer, not life sentence.
Learn to enjoy work.*
—Laurie Macintosh

34

Voice of Customer

Ignore at your own risk and peril

Customer is the least acknowledged species in the business circles, only few companies like Amazon, Maruti, Tatas (just an example, there will certainly be many more) understand the importance and the value of the voice of customer. Most of the utilities and service companies including banks hardly understand the voice of customer leave aside the body language which conveys more than what is articulated by words. Let me reproduce what Jeff Bezos[1], owner of Amazon statement on the customer:

- The best customer service is when customer does not need to call you, does not need to talk to you. It just works.
- Don't Just Listen to your customers, understand them.
- If you make customers unhappy in the physical world, they might each tell six friends. If you make customers unhappy on the Internet, they can each tell six thousand.

Importance of voice of customer is well understood by companies who are on growth path. They understand very well that their existence, survival and growth are due to the customer. They understand very well that all the improvement plans in the product, price, service, quality logistics, cost, packaging, and logistics will come from customer and not from consultants or manuals or the product manufacturers.

Customer will give unadulterated, unbiased feedback on all parameters mentioned above. Feedback good or bad will land on you whether you like it or not. Good companies encourage direct feed back to the managers who can take it as a gift. Not many managers can accept the feedback if it borders on severe criticism, leave aside acting on that. In not so customer friendly companies, most of the feedback is pushed under the carpet for fear of explanations and then starts the downhill journey of the team, product and company. Be grateful to the customer for his voice, text or body signals on the product, price, specifications or any other service aspects. He is doing a favour, accept it and be thankful to him. No other feedback from a person who has not spent money on your product will be useful. Figure out ways and means to capture the voice of the customer. Your CEO will get shaken up by the feedback.

1, Jeff Bezos is the founder of Amazon, a company whose market capitalization is around 1 trillion USD. He is the richest person on this planet with personal wealth worth $143.3 billion, according to Forbes, which is just over $50 billion more than the next richest person alive, Microsoft co-founder Bill Gates, who is currently worth over $93 billion.

**Encourage and accept feedback
as a valuable gift!**

I think swagger is a confidence. It is a confidence of you knowing that you work hard for your success. A lot of times, you cannot develop swagger if you have not worked hard to succeed.

—Amar'e Stoudemire

35

Swagger Index
Keep under check

By way of few rapid achievements in early stages of your career, has your Swagger index (Read Arrogance, Attitude of I am always right, not able to see others view point) gone high? Pinch yourself and figure it out. Seek feedback from your most trusted source who is your sounding board. This can happen to anyone, it's very natural. Strength lies in noticing it and taking corrective action. Few early symptoms of swagger index going high are

- Always last or late for the meeting.
- Using derogatory words in email or face to face communication.
- Dressing in a manner that defies the norms.
- No patience to hear what other person is saying and reacting before his completing the argument.
- Not giving due respect to females.
- Not getting up while shaking hands and looking other way while shaking hand or without an eye contact.
- Cracking irrelevant jokes and expecting others to laugh.
- Raising your voice every now and then.
- Treating subordinate staff with disrespect.
- Addressing people with self-discovered nick names and not the real names.

Recently I went to an office of a reputed company to meet a very senior official. Let us call him Mr. S (the real Swagger).The time, date was as per the convenience of Mr S, whom I was to meet, and agenda was also known and documented a day ahead. Meeting should not have lasted for more than half an hour. On arrival at the reception, I was told that he is busy, and I need to wait. While I kept myself busy with my reading on kindle while waiting, suddenly I realized that it is more than 45 minutes, I have been waiting. I just got up and told the person at reception in most polite manner that I am leaving and will come back if needed. He immediately called up Mr S and instant response was that I can go to meet him in his cabin past few security checks on the floors.

Mr S was sitting pretty in his chair with no possible signs of his being awfully busy and not having had any meeting earlier. He did not bother to get up to shake hand and his apology to start the meeting late was fake and posturing. Now when you meet a person for the first time with this set up, obviously discussions will be muted, and one would leave with a bad taste. One will remember this for all times to come and label Mr S accordingly. Your future interactions will be guarded with due care for your time management.

During the course of short meeting he continued to attend unimportant calls on land line, mobile phone thereby making the meeting as waste of time for both of us.

He saved his swagger index a little by getting up to shake hand when I was leaving and it was least expected. One can always have the option of:

- ▶ Going out of your room and telling the visitor in person of delay, it helps and no one minds.
- ▶ Reschedule the meeting ahead of time.
- ▶ Put other meetings on hold for a while.

At the end of day making people wait for whatever reason is the most arrogant behaviour especially if it is an agreed and scheduled meeting.

One can argue that Mr. S may not have interest in the agenda, but then it was discussed and agreed ahead of time.

Now this Swagger index going up will bring you down faster in people's mind and your ability to deal with others will become increasingly difficult as the time passes.

ACTIONABLE   **Do not do anything which will hurt you if reciprocated!**

You change your business plan to expect and adapt to changes in the marketplace.

— Jon Feltheimer

36

Anticipate

See beyond your nose!

With experience, we all professionals get used to lots of planning on work front. Planning is based on many things which include:

- ► Your boss's agenda for next week, be it travel or any of his meetings and resultant expectations from you.
- ► Deliverables on daily, weekly and monthly basis.
- ► Your personal travel plans for official work.
- ► Industry events which need to be attended.
- ► Deadlines approaching for payment of various bills.
- ► Dates for completing your or other's appraisals.
- ► Plan for holidays, booking tickets.
- ► Family needs.

Anticipating anything ahead of time is an attribute which will give you rich dividends. Examples given above are of routine nature, but what saves the major embarrassment is your ability to anticipate small and very insignificant things which make or mar your personal and team's reputation. Examples are

- ► Not rehearsing your ppt and finding that it is not coming on the projector for some time when audience is waiting, this is very common and often.
- ► PA system does not work when required.
- ► Not having wheel chaired enabled venues for special guests.

▶ Poor estimation of guest numbers for an event (more or less either way is troublesome from minimum guaranteed payment commitment).

▶ Not preparing and improper finalization of sequence of events for a function.

▶ Wrongly spelt names on name plates.

▶ Use of inappropriate words while addressing teams.

▶ Not available on the appointed day and time and not communicating your absence to the guest.

▶ Not checking the travel time before commencing your local journey.

▶ Not looking the weather forecast for a proposed event day.

▶ Deciding to hold the events on a day or time not favourable to a community or a section of people.

▶ Not starting the functions on time.

▶ Not able to finish your speech or presentation in time and asked to cut it short.

▶ Not knowing the guests food preferences.

Ability to mentally map all the expected hurdles and find ways to handle them if they pop up will save lots of embarrassment. Detailing is the key to success. Developing a minute to minute program and documenting it with roles and responsibilities fixed will give you all joy. Do this as a routine for personal issues as well or get fired by your spouse more often than you really deserve.

ACTIONABLE **Always have full dress rehearsal for major events. Eliminate bottlenecks!**

Failure is just the opportunity to begin again more intelligently.

—Henry Ford

37

Handle Failure

Start again with a smile

*I*n a long career you are bound to face failures some time or other. Earlier you fail in your career better it will be as consequences of your failures will be limited and corrective actions can be taken care of. Your understanding of the causes of failure will be immediate and you will have plenty of time for correction in remaining part of your career. I am not suggesting that you fail, but do try hard to innovate, take risk: you never know things may turn out in your favour and you have life changing moments before the interval.

Reasons for failure can be many as explained below:

- ► Your poor personal-attitude to the work, you are not being 100%.
- ► Market going against you for reasons of volatility, supply demand situation bringing the excess supply into system.
- ► Boss not in line with your thoughts or not aligned to overall objective.
- ► Sudden regulatory changes impacting the core of the business.
- ► Delays in project execution because of vendors, contractors or suppliers.
- ► Team has issues working together.
- ► Poor visualization of customer's needs & expectations.
- ► Inadequate market intelligence on product, price, promotion, cost, quality logistics, and service parameters.
- ► Your own customer becoming your competitor.

The consequences of failure at senior level can be huge and can put back the organisation by few years. All these failures if well arrested before damage reaches an unbearable level are greatest lessons of life. They will go a long way with you for all times to come. Long years of job careers are full of ups and downs and failure is a part. Unable to reach the targeted sales or complete the project in time or realize the money from the market or stop the revenue leakage in the system by way of inefficient sourcing or price the product at optimum level or service the customer are some examples of failures which happen day in day out in professional life. You should be able to notice the impending failure ahead of time and share it with your team for corrective action. This way you can save the situation, but this does not happen all the time.

What is important and significant is what do you do after the failure. How quickly you can move away from that experience of having failed. Do you:

- ▶ Remain in denial mode that it wasn't because of you?
- ▶ Blame the environment.
- ▶ Blame the seniors or all other department, peer group for not providing the support which was required.
- ▶ Do you look around for a scapegoat to fix responsibility?
- ▶ Undertake a deep dive in trying to figure out as to what happened and remain engaged in this exercise with full team of yours for a considerable time.
- ▶ Resolve that no new initiatives will be undertaken henceforth, and you will only maintain status quo in the business.

Just move on cheerfully, take the lessons on its stride, smile at yourself, say thank you life for the experience taught and catch up with your momentum sooner than later.

Look at the way failures are handled by most of the sports persons. Senior sports person takes each day without any reference to the days gone by where they may have failed miserably, say out on the first ball, or going for good number of runs in few overs, not able to complete the race in time, not able to lift the weight as per requirement. Just leave that thought of failure, let it not occupy your mind even for a second. Your ability to forget that sooner than later, matters. Even if people remind you of that day of failure, move on; do not engage in any discussion whatsoever. It's all done and dusted.

Jack Ma the richest person in china and founder of Alibaba had following failures in his life:

1. Failed four times in Primary and middle school.
2. Rejected 10 times from Harvard.
3. Failed entrance exam twice before being admitted to Hangzhou's university.
4. Rejected by Police, KFC and finally started as a teacher @12 USD per month.

Mohammed Gauri fought with Prithvi Raj Chauhan 17 times and possibly on 18th attempt Prithvi Raj Chauhan appreciating his commitment, refused to fight again and asked him to go back and declare that he has won the war.

ACTIONABLE   **Restart afresh after failure. You just figured out how not to do something!**

Letting go of toxic people is a major step
towards being happier
—Anonymous

38

Choose Company within your Company

So critical for your career

You have landed in a job you deserve and in the company you were longing.

Or

You have had a good break through from your existing job and have switched to a company which is best in the industry.

Or

You had change of location and the department as well because of routine transfer or elevation.

Every company has set of people:

- ▶ Who can be differentiated based on merit, attitude, and commitment to the work place.
- ▶ Who are front runners.
- ▶ Whose emotional intelligence is way above others.
- ▶ Whose etiquette level is worth emulating.
- ▶ Whose smiles are infectious.
- ▶ Whose sense of dressing is worth looking at again and again.

Your team will also have set of people who differ in their attitudes, integrity and many other factors which affect the results, deliverables and enthusiasm of the company. Your first capability test is choosing the right people for your network within your company you are working for. Be aware that you do not:

- ▶ Land up with the persons with doubtful integrity.
- ▶ Associate with persons who shirk work and are readymade excuse inventors.
- ▶ Spend time with persons for whom world is falling all the time and will not let you embark on any of the innovations, new initiatives.
- ▶ Come near the person who laughed few years ago.
- ▶ Persons for whom bitching about the boss is the biggest past time and most enjoyable time.
- ▶ Persons who say yes to anything and everything (had a colleague who would say yes even before boss has finished his sentence or completely defined the work proposition).
- ▶ Groups formed based on religion, caste etc.

The above few criterions are strict no and out of bounds for personal growth. Choose your company within the company you work for with utmost care as your entire growth and reputation will depend upon the company you chose.

I have seen many careers getting destroyed as the person was found in the company of not so appropriate, upright persons. You should quit the company of doubtful integrity person in the first place without a second thought. You should quit the company of the person who does not have courage of convictions the company of persons who lie on small matters the company of persons who posture all the time, and the company of persons who fudge facts and numbers.

Always remember 80/20 rule. 20 percent people or customers drive the 80 percent business. Choose to be with right people and right company in the company you work.

ACTIONABLE   **Choose right people to be with. It makes difference!**

*The journey of a thousand miles
begins with one step.*
—Lao Tzu

39

Commence your Journey

First step is the most difficult

Never you will find full answers to all your concerns, questions to anything new you want to undertake either in personal or professional life. As an example if you want to buy a house or build a house on your own, you will start your due diligence at some time to zero down on your budget, location, size of the house, floor, investments of your own, and amount of loan, builder and many other such things. In all fairness, once all your questions are answered only then you should step out and close the deal once for all. This never happens in real life.

You would be exceptionally lucky or blessed if this happens to you or has already happened to you. Now let's look at your variables. You can't apply for loan, unless deal is finalized. Unless deal is finalized the budget clarity won't come. Deal can be finalized only if you know the complete market of real estate availability, supply and demand, possible time zones of occupying the house and many other such factors. Lack of clarity and indecisiveness can lead to undue delays in your possessing the house and will only mean extra costs by way of rent, enhanced EMIs etc. Your ability to payback will also be reduced if you lose time as you grow older.

Assuming on professional front a new product project is to be established which has gestation period of say 24-36 months. All mid to large size investments do take so much of time. Multiple issues here come into play before decision is taken. In today's VUCA (Volatile, Uncertain, Complex and Uncertain) world what you decide today may not be best of the decisions after say a year or two. Market, environment, interest rate and such like important factors can undergo a change in a matter of months.

Once you have reasonable clarity on the various factors which come into play for taking a decision, you should commence your journey on the personal and professional front.

This will need some important commitment financial or otherwise signalling your intent to move forward in that direction. No sooner you start taking actions, things will start falling into place. You will engage yourself in much more serious exercise of execution from that day.

Certain decisions in personal and professional life need to be forced upon oneself once intent to achieve something in life is clear in the mind. Like buying a house, you will need to crystallize, build consensus in the family as to where you want to live from available choices on the horizon. There is no point procrastinating for long time for possible locations or solutions which will never be a reality in few years to come. If you engage yourself in such acts, you will miss the bus and repent in leisure for all times to come. This story of repent will be a favourite talk of yours in the senior's club when you reach there. Turn this into story of achievement for later part of life by forcing yourself into a decision.

ACTIONABLE   **Check your ability to procrastinate. Put a limit!**

Must acknowledge many persons besides my wife
Meenakshi and son Siddhant Chhabra

My grateful thanks are due to:

Swarup Rani Khullar
Vinod Bala Dua
Madhu Chhabra
Gaurav and Pamela
Dr Pradeep Chowbey
Professor Sandeep Puri
Manju and Chand Mehta
Brij and Surinder Kapania
Dr Sangita and Himanshu Kapania
Gurdeep and Pranjali Malhotra
Late Rakesh and Jaya Khullar
Dr Rajesh and Dr Poonam Khullar
Ranjeev and Rachna Mehta
Duggal
Rajeev and Nisha Khullar
Meenu and Vikas Kanwar
Kartik Dua
Amit and Meenal
Anurag and Vinita
Amit and Natasha
Amit and Parul
Gulshan Suneja
Satish GK
CK Tiwari
Naresh Nayyar
Dr RK Malhotra
Makrand Nene
Rajiv Ailawadi
Rajiv Mathur

Akhil Joshi
RR Shastri
DK Sharma
Subodh Dakwale
M. Kali Krishna
Avinash Verma
R Nanda Kumar
Bhuwan Joshi
Alok Roy
Satyendra Sahai
Rabinder Nanda
Gudipati Kodandram
Subodh Goyal
SK Gupta
Satish Sharma
RV Prabhu
Mathew
Abhay Singh
Prudhvi
Anindya
Sukanta Bhattacharjee
Dipdyuti Chowdhury
Sangram Mishra
Saroj Kant Roy
Rajesh Pathak
Angshuman
Syed Fazayal Shabbir
Vipin Pandey
Rajesh Sharma

Rajiv Dewan

Rajinder Kohli

Pradeep Pangasa

Nirmal Mahendale

SK Gandhi

Sudhir Batra

Sohinder Singh

DK Arora

Preet Pal Matharu

Uday Chand

K Sambhamurthy

Praveen Kumar

Amish Shah

Sanjiv Bhalla

Narayan Bhatra

Atul Mathur

Saurabh Mishra

Anirudh Narula

Atul and Shruti Kumar

Manish Singh

Mukesh Panhotra

Harshit Sinha

Vibhu Saxena

Yogesh

Vishal Saxena

Dilpreet Singh

Vanu Wadhwa

Udit Saboo

Anurita Ghosh

Pramod Patil

Khim Raj Bhatt

Bhanu Pratap

Suresh Sirohi

Sanjeev Divedi

Gaurav Gupta

Varun Pahwa

Prashant

Ankush Juneja

Prodyut Majhi

Aseem Pratap Singh

Sajjad Khan

Dibeyendu Deepak

Vinod Kumat

Earlier Publications

UNCORK YOURSELF NOT BOTTLES a nonfiction book authored by Pradeep Chhabra is available on line on Amazon, Flipkart, Notionpress both in paperback and as eBook.